A household name through his many
television shows, including *London*
Night Out at the Casino and *The Tom O'Connor*
Show, Tom O'Connor is one of the most sought-
after entertainers in the country and one of Britain's
funniest comedians. With seven popular game
shows, including *Name That Tune*, *Gambit*, *Pass-*
word and *Cross Wits*, to his credit, Tom continues
to undertake a heavy schedule of concerts, cabaret
and after-dinner engagements around the country.

He lives in Berkshire with his wife Pat.

Also by Tom O'Connor

FROM THE WOOD TO THE TEES
THE WORLD'S WORST JOKES

TOM O'CONNOR

TAKE A FUNNY TURN

An Autobiography

WARNER BOOKS

A *Warner* Book

First published in Great Britain in 1994 by Robson Books Ltd
This edition published in 1995 by Warner Books

Copyright © 1994 Tom O'Connor

A CIP catalogue record for this book
is available from the British Library.

ISBN 0 7515 1481 0

Printed in England by Clays Ltd, St Ives plc

Warner Books
A Division of
Little, Brown and Company (UK)
Brettenham House
Lancaster Place
London WC2E 7EN

For you, Amy, because you light up my life

1

Where do I begin? I know that's a song title, but don't worry, I'm not going to sing – although strangely enough that's how the whole thing began. That's what drove this potential policeman to become a TV personality, through many diversions – railway worker, docker, schoolteacher, butcher, baker. But hang on! Let's start at the beginning.

When your first-ever recollection is of being carried into an air raid shelter – the noise, the screams, the smell of burning buildings, the nearness of death – then life is a bonus. You learn to find fun where you can, maybe not to laugh at everything, but certainly at some of the things that otherwise might frighten you.

Believe me, wars are a lot funnier than they are serious. I've lived through a few and still smile at 'loose lips sink ships', 'careless talk costs lives', 'be like dad – keep mum'.

I suppose Liverpool in 1939 is as close to World War 2 as you could want to be. My Dad was away in the army, the blitz was in full swing and young O'Connor was dragged screaming into the fray. Most new babies look alike, I know, but when they're all wearing gas masks they are identical! So from these beginnings grew the me who collected pieces of shrapnel from out of the tarmac-ed streets, who learned to recognise aeroplanes, friend and foe, from sound and silhouette, who learned to eat when and wherever he could, to respect dignity and inner strength in other people. But mostly to keep on the funny side of life, to go to hell in a handcart, but go there laughing.

APR warden: Why are you leaving the shelter?
Lady: I'm going to get my false teeth.
APR warden: Listen love, they're dropping bombs not sand-
                   wiches.
Lady: Away ye scmernak! (I never did find out what
                   that meant – something Irish.)

That was my grandmother, Biddie McGrath, Irish and proud of it and one of the great abusers of the English language: 'I remember the good old days. You'd could make a meal out of nothing if you had the stuff.'

'How's your new teeth, gran?'

'I'm leaving them out till I get used to them.'

'Thomas! You fall off that wall and break your legs, don't come running to me!'

Biddie was widowed in World War 1 and then met and married Billy McGrath, an Irish 'coal heaver'. Heavers were men who shovelled coal out of and into railway trucks. Billy was a star – a two hander who could clear any wagon left or right handed. A man of enormous strength, great compassion and, knowing my grandmother, immense patience. I loved my grandad, but in all the years I knew him I never understood one word he said.

Whether it was the lack of teeth, the deep Irish twang, or the Guinness, all my young ears could pick up would be statements like: 'Harn ee far ay noor ack friney – huh?'

And I would have to guess by the inflection in the voice whether the answer was yes or no. Mostly out of desperation I usually got it right: to get it wrong was to risk the back of his hand. But I remember grandad as the smell of a pipe, the tired but smiling eyes, the gnarled fingers and the shuddering laugh, particularly at any mishap that befell grandma. 'Ween fet outd lute fan dellar may' (followed by hysterical laughter) was his reaction when the parish priest sat on her best hat.

My gran had many hats – twenty plus, I reckon – but never wore them. She preferred the head scarf or shawl that was popular in those days. In fact the only time I saw her in a hat was in a photograph she treasured – so much so, that she ran back into a burning building to rescue it. At the time it seemed to me the most ridiculous of actions, until 1992 when my wife Pat and I were running from a 1400 lb bomb in Belfast and looked down to see what we'd instinctively snatched from our hotel room. I had a mobile telephone, while Pad had 'saved' a cheque made out to Barclaycard!

But I digress, back to grandmother. Biddie McGrath had ready wit and all the Irish ways. She also had a cure for anything – even for diseases that didn't exist. She had a medicine cabinet full of bottles, all different colours and types. They contained liquids that only Dr Jekyll would recognise – some actually smoked when you took the lid off. Lotions, potions, cure-alls and remedies that had been there so long they would be condemned by today's health services. But in those days they were a source of relief, if only psychological, to the true believers.

Gran could cure anything and some of the cures were stunningly simple. When my cousin Michael caught German measles she put my cousin Donald and me in bed with him to 'take the disease off him'. The theory was that one child passed it on to another in a never ending chain or until some kid in the middle of nowhere caught it and had no one to pass it on to! Somewhere there's a child who's still got every ailment under the sun.

But of course to cure ills was not the only task for grandmas: they had to try to prevent them by nourishing the inner child. And this had to be done in a period of austerity, indeed virtual poverty. Not for us steak or lamb cutlets, pork chops or fresh eggs. Powdered eggs from America (thanks, Mr Roosevelt), plenty of potatoes and a little meat from hitherto unexploited parts of animals. Pig's feet, knuckle of beef, oxtails, neck end of lamb. I grew up believing that animals were really full of bones with a loose layer of skin thrown over. But who cares what's in the food if the stomach is full? Who cares that bombs are dropping when you've never known a time when they weren't?

Who needs purpose built toys when there are so many real substitutes – shrapnel, cartridge cases, army badges. I remember getting into serious trouble as a three-year-old because I'd taken my dad's army bayonet to play in the street! It almost ruined dad's leave, but made me a big man round our way.

It's always happy days when you're young and learning new things. I learned that radios worked from acid batteries which frequently had to be 'topped up' at the local store. When you've no electricity, and only gas for lighting, it really is the eighth wonder of the world to find a cube-shaped bottle full of fluid that can make voices come out of a box on the sideboard.

'Get those batteries topped up, and when you come back don't shake them or you'll mix the programmes up!' Gran was at it again. And another time: 'Ask the butcher for an oxtail – and see if he'll leave the legs on for you.'

Even funerals were not safe from her garbled outlook on life. On someone remarking that the deceased looked happy, Gran replied: 'Yes, he died in his sleep and he doesn't know he's dead yet. If he wakes up in the morning the shock will kill him!'

Barney Rooney once said to me: 'Little 'un, promise me you won't let your Gran organise my send off.' His send off was his funeral, and he meant it when he made me promise. Barney was a tiny man – certainly not more than five feet tall: a real diddyman. His size inspired the comic imagination of his friends: 'He's the last man in Liverpool to know when it's raining.' 'He's the only docker with turnups in his underpants.' 'Could be a hod carrier for Lego.' 'When he gets annoyed in the pub he stamps around under the tables.' And so on.

Barney was used to this and could laugh it off with a humour all of his own. A humour that came, not from being resignedly small, but from having to take the world on toe to toe. I've seen it since in many people, in many places where there is poverty, adversity, deep sorrow, loss of life. It's the ability to shine through the darkness and laugh at things just to prove you're not afraid of them. It's a gift that raises mankind above the rest and gives us pride.

Barney had it. Barney needed it. Though not because of his stature. Barney was unlucky. The world's most unlucky man. If it was raining soup Barney would be standing with a fork in his hand. In all the years I knew the man I never saw him win a hand of cards. Each Friday Uncle Dan ('Doc'), Uncle Dennis, Dad, Barney and sometimes others would play poker in Biddy's kitchen. Bottled Guinness and Woodbines were the order of the day and the banter would be free. Dad never smoked or drank and Barney would say 'Paddy, in thirty years time you'll be lying in bed dying of nothing!' (Fifty years on he's still fit and well.)

The stakes were small – pennies in old coins – but the concentration was intense. Cards were counted and memorised by all, but Barney's ace in the hole was religion. On his person he'd carry rosary beads, Lourdes medals and small prayer books. He even took to sitting on a Bible (he said to give him more height) and every time he drew a card he'd say 'That's a Godsend'. But Barney never won a hand.

Barney never smiled. Some say because, amidst all his other misfortunes, his wife ran off with a GI. Apparently Barney kept a light burning in the window for years but she never returned. Although the lads reckoned she did return once when he was out but when she saw the size of the electric bill she ran off again!

Such was the stuff of my youth – funny people, funny situations – so many things to learn.

The docks played a major part in my early days because they provided work for virtually all the men in the family. Uncle Tom – my mum's brother – was in charge of machinery at Gladstone Dock and was a 'stand-in' dad while my real one was fighting in Germany. Uncle Tom was a big man prematurely grey (as I would become): 'Big man, white hair' the Chinese crew men called him. He was an ace footballer, snooker player and, according to my mum, an ace locksmith. I never saw him pick a lock although in frustration I've seen him smash a few beyond repair!

He showed me DIY tips that never appeared in any manual then. To make do without a drill or brace and bit he would heat a poker in the fire and burn a hole through wood! He would clean bicycle wheels and gear chains with penetrating oil and coat them with Vaseline to prevent rust. He would search for punctures by immersing inner tubes in tin baths full of water.

Uncle Tom did these bicycle repairs and many other wondrous things while never leaving the fireside! He would plonk toolbox, nails, bicycle and all in front of the fire no matter what else was going on in the room. Visitors could only remark on his prowess.

'That's nothing,' I used to think, 'you should see the shelves and cupboards he's put up!' Yes, Uncle Tom built things to last and never used anything less than a 4 inch nail – even when hanging a calendar. I followed his admirable lead and can proudly boast that there are houses in which I've lived that have shelves and other wooden fitments that are just as massive as the structural timbers.

Uncle Tom loved music. He could sing. He could also whistle through his teeth (a feat I never could master through years of trying), and he liked to be surrounded by music, which he was prone to embellish by rhythmic tapping of teaspoons on saucer and cup. Once I visited his 'den' at the docks and heard him and his team tendering 'Dixie'. It was cacophonous, it was irritating, it was dire, it was many things – but it certainly wasn't music. Nevertheless it suited the dockers, and that was a lesson to me. Never assume that what's good for you is good for all. The public may not know what they like but they like what they know.

If Uncle Tom's music was bad, mum's was good. She played piano and sang soprano-ish. To be truthful, the piano playing was fine except that the left hand occasionally left a lot to be desired. None the less she made fair fist of 'My Mother's Eyes', 'Little Town in the Old County Down' and other imperishable classics, although 'Bless this House' was always a trifle iffy. The main thing was that mum and the family generally loved to entertain and were not afraid to do so in front of crowds – a trait that passed on to me, I'm happy to say, and to my kids and grandkids.

'Son, if you wake up in the morning every day's your birthday.' So said the great Bill Shankly. And, like him, I learned to believe that when you're young, fit and clear-headed, there's no limit to what you can discover and to what you can achieve.

In Miss Leeson's class at St James's Infants' School we learned our times tables by chanting them parrot fashion ('once two is two, two twos are four'). But I would test myself in my spare time by reciting them backwards. I read books many times over – we had so few that it was never a chore. After four or five readings I found I could remember whole passages word for word. Little did I know it, but I was training myself in what became a photographic memory with a difference. Not only could I retain whole chunks of words, but if necessary I could learn passages for a short period only and then totally forget them – an ideal gift when dealing with 'one-off'. TV or radio scripts.

Yes, unknowingly, young O'Connor was grooming himself as a showbusiness performer. When school playtimes were rained off I would entertain the class with a story I'd learned. Robin Hood in rhyme was my best. So while Marty Rimmer was the only mixed infant who could turn his eyelids inside out, Tommy O'Connor could weave a spell of words.

'I wasn't very good at school – I was there three years before I got a tick!' 'I was the only one in our class who failed milk!' 'I was teacher's pet – she kept me in a cage at the back of the classroom!' All these lines formed part of my act over the years, but none of them was true. I loved school and was good at maths and English. My retentive memory helped me through exams even in subjects I didn't like, such as, history, geography, organic chemistry and Latin. I remember a comic line that went: 'Forte dux fel flat in gutta'. This is just a phonetic rendering, you understand, and I've no idea what it means, but it has been lodged firmly in my mind these forty years. So has:

> There was a young Scotsman called Sandy
> Who went into a bar for a shandy
> When he lifted his kilt to wipe what he'd spilt
> The barman said, 'Blimey, that's handy!'

Whose immortal lines are these – Max Miller's, maybe, or Billy Bennett's? Anyway my young brain just soaked them up and now I can recall them at will: 'Barman, what's the quickest way to Fazackerly Hospital?' 'Drink that big fella's pint.'

'You remind me of a man.'
'What man?'
'The man with the power.'
'What power?'
'The power of Hoodoo.'
'Hoodoo?'
'You do.'
'Do what?'
'Remind me of a man' ... etc.

This epic round was recited by Cary Grant in one of the thousands of films I watched in my younger days. Movies were a youngster's release from the drab and dreary streets of post-war Bootle. They transported me to exotic or romantic locations all over the world – the jungle, the Bowery, the Wild West, ancient China, medieval Britain, Sherwood Forest. I've been there and seen it all through the fascinated eyes of a child. I saw and believed and loved and cried but, most importantly, I remembered.

It began with the Saturday morning pictures. In the late 1940s everyone was an ABC Minor. We had our own song:

We are the boys and girls well known
As the minors of the ABC.
And every Saturday we line up to see the films [pronounced 'fillums']
And we shout aloud with glee.

It was true, we'd queue for hours to enter the hallowed halls of the Gainsborough cinema – though when we were inside very few of us watched the screen. We'd run about fighting and throwing things. Spraying the auditorium with disinfectant ('Here comes Mr Flit') failed to shut our mouths. The soundtrack was impossible to hear over the noise of screaming kids. And the picture was regularly interrupted by series of numbers, circles and crosses going backwards, or by film turning brown from the middle outwards. But it was fun, and the more exciting movies provided us with fantasies of what we'd like to be in adulthood: *Hopalong Cassidy*, *Flash Gordon*, *Sabu the Elephant Boy* and many others that today's kids would instantly banish with the remote button.

I can remember plenty of occasions when there were at least 300 kids in the picture house, only twenty of whom had paid (the others having come through the push bar exit in the gents). We'd buy four penn'orth of winkles and a pin to eat them with. Then we'd put the empty shells on the wooden floor of the cinema and every time someone in the movie shook hands we'd crunch them under our shoes. That was fun but it was a red card offence, earning immediate expulsion and a permanent ban, at least until you changed your appearance enough to fool old Ben, the chief usher and owner of a raucous voice and gammy leg.

I've seen 'Ben' many times in the years since: he's in every car park, he's every hotel night porter, he's a waiter in your least favourite restaurant. And he's in my act.

Saturday mornings were an adventure at the Gainsborough, but my real thrills came in the evenings when two films were shown. 'Sun/Mon-Tue-Wed/Thur-Fri-Sat' reminded me of a Chinese family but referred to the three changes of programme per week, making six full-length films in all. In those days the programmes played continuously without an interval, so I could stay through three showings per day. Sometimes my mum would bring a parcel of sandwiches and the usherette would bring them to my seat (there's service for you!). By staying all day and evening I learned by heart some wonderful routines by Bob Hope, Syd Caesar and other brilliant comics – all good stuff to stock the comic brain.

Sometimes we favoured other picture houses in the neighbourhood, mainly the Palace (or bug house) and the Sun Hall (called 'the Ranch' because of the number of western films it showed). It was in the Sun Hall that I heard this arresting exchange between two ladies:

'You know that creepy bloke that's always in here at the weekend?'

'Yeah.'

'Well, the other night he sat beside me and put his hand right up my skirt.'

'My God! Not the green one with the floral pattern?'

And recalling that one brings others to mind, such as:

'My son's at university taking medicine.'

'Oh, and is it doing him any good?'

And more recently:

'About the Volvo, dear. There's good news and bad news. The good news is, the air bag works.'

Ladies are without doubt the more intelligent sex, but have you ever seen a man wearing a shirt that buttons up the back? Ladies are allowed to say anything they like – even if long term it doesn't make sense:

'Billy's having trouble with his head – it's been off and on all day.'

'Doctor, can you do something with his face – he's had it a while and it's spreading?'

Or the celebrated letter from a mother to the schoolmaster:

'Johnny couldn't come today because he hasn't been. I've given him something to make him go and as soon as he's been he'll come.'

I'll return to schools and mothers' sayings later in the narrative, as both made great impressions on me and my act. But for the while let me close this chapter with a few words about the woman who helped form my character and inspired my quest for knowledge and excellence – my mother, Theresa (née Stack) O'Connor, who loved all forms of art, music and literature. A very intelligent and widely read lady whose two joys in life were giving or receiving entertainment, and who had one of the heartiest laughs I've ever heard. Oh, that she were a hundredfold in every audience – there'd be no hard nights for comics.

But to me her greatest gift was her speed of thought and almost simultaneous speed of speech. We had a lady two doors down who was known as 'borrowing Bertha' because she was always on the scrounge. Here's a typical request of hers:

'Could you possibly lend me half a dozen eggs, two pounds of flour, a pound of sugar, two pounds of currants and a pound of butter? Only I've found some soda and I was thinking of baking a cake.' There's no answer to that sort of approach I hear you cry, but witness a typical Theresa O'Connor retort:

Bertha: Could you lend me your clothes line for a couple of days or so?

Mother: I'm sorry, but I'm using it to tie up some loose sawdust.

Bertha: You can't tie up sawdust with a clothes line.

Mother: It's amazing what you can do with a clothes line when you don't want to lend it out!

Hats off to you mum – would you were alive to read that exploit for yourself.

2

When I was a ten-year-old anxiously awaiting the 11-plus exam and hoping for a grammar school place, I had to write an essay on 'what I would like to be when I grow up'. Unlike my classmates, who chose jobs like train driver, airline pilot and even clown, I settled for policeman, mainly because of the authority that those days went with the uniform, and the respect that the community gave the local copper.

However, despite this 'official' preference, and despite pressure by my parents to become a priest, or at least a doctor, secretly I always longed to work on the docks. With my strong mathematical bent, I reckoned I could work in the accountancy branch of Mersey Docks and Harbour Board. Why this deep desire? Admittedly my father was a docker, but that was not the real reason. To understand the mind of this child you must know that in the 1950s, '60s and '70s Liverpool dockers were a breed alone. Like the gunfighters of old, the gladiators, or even the golf caddies of today, the dockers had their own way of life, their own code of honour, their own rules and even their own language! I used to regale my classmates in junior and grammar school with the nicknames of some of my father's mates: the Weightlifter ('I'll wait here while you lift that'), the Olympic

Torch ('he never goes out'), the Bald Rabbit (he gets on the bus and says 'I've got no fur'), and so on.

I worked amongst these men as an eighteen-year-old student awaiting a college place and I learned how wondrous their life was. The boss of my gang was nicknamed 'Harry the Horse', presumably after the Damon Runyon character in *Guys and Dolls*.

One day the foreman came round and said: 'Where's Harry the Horse?' And my pal Stevie replied, 'We haven't seen head nor tail of him all day.' Wouldn't you love an opportunity to come out with a line like that?

In those days there was a system on the docks called 'The welt', whereby a gang of four would do the work of six, giving two men a day off. What time and motion experts would do about that the Lord only knows. It reminded me of the Irish story of the bloke who walked off the job on the building site, and Paddy said to the foreman, 'Sir, you can replace him with me brother Sean – he can do the work of two men'. 'If that's the case,' said the foreman, 'send him tomorrow and you're fired.'

But all in all the docks were the place to be. I recall an occasion at the North One Gladstone Dock when a gang of men spotted a rat amongst the hold cargo on a ship. 'That's it,' said the leading ganger, 'we're on strike until we get vermin money – infestation pay.' The bosses agreed and offered them £1 extra a day plus a cat. 'Get off,' they replied. 'We want £2 and the pied piper!' (Later I heard of a similar problem at the docks in Dublin where crews had to unload a cargo of toilet seats. They demanded 'Embarrassment money'.

These and a myriad other tales would help to flesh out my early showbiz club act, though at the time I merely dismissed them as good fun and something to remember to tell over a pint at the pub. We had one legendary occurrence when a gang on night work found an unmarked keg aboard a ship and, just to check it, they broke a hole in the side with a hook. The liquid which flowed out was tested by the 'sick pigeon' (he's always in the loft) and found to be pure alcohol – if a little sedimentary. The boys drank their fill, mixing the strange fluid with orange juice from another cargo. They lay in a stupor till morning, when a couple of men from the school of tropical medicine arrived to pick up the keg – which contained a pickled monkey.

Of course, there were also times of personal discomfort and even disaster. At one time I was employed by Liverpool Warehousing Company to sample and weigh cocoa beans. This entailed loading five sacks of beans on to a scale and recording their weight and grade. Depending on the amount of cargo moved from quayside to warehouse we could earn a bonus, called 'tonnage'. Each gang had a checker, a man who recorded the details in a book using an indelible pencil. He was easy to spot – he generally had a purple nose from drinking brandy, screwed up eyes from trying to read his own writing and a purple tongue and bottom lip from licking his pencil. Our checker was called 'the Home Secretary' (if you didn't keep an eye on him he'd sneak off home).

The Home Secretary was slow on a good day; on bad days he was stationary. So I suggested a short cut to tonnage money. Having discovered that the average weight of five bags of beans was one hundredweight, I suggested he work from a 'fictitious mean' – a mathematical term which induced a glazed look in his eyes.

'Look,' said I, 'let's assume that every five bags weigh 112 pounds. Then instead of recording the weight of every bag and adding them together, we simply weigh five bags at a time and record the amount by which they differ from 112 pounds. For instance, we record 114 pounds as + 2, or 111 pounds as − 1.'

This totally lost the checker but was greeted with great enthusiasm by the rest of the gang. So began my still-remembered journey towards dismissal. With my system, we were soon clearing the shed at a rate of knots and we got to the point where we were weighing cargo straight from the ship. This meant that the sacks of beans were not being allowed to stand to allow moisture to seep away before they were weighed. In other words the beans lost weight while in transit by lorry.

At the end of my last week we all had a pay packet of £19, but we'd lost an invisible one and a half tons to moisture – and I took the rap for being 'a smart arse'. But I will always thank those times for my humour, my quick wit and my realisation that a smile can lighten the heaviest of burdens.

It reminds me of the union delegate addressing the dockers at strike-bound Pier Head in Liverpool: 'Men, we've stood the bosses on their heads. They've agreed to double our wages [cheers!], backdate the rise eighteen months [more cheers!] and in future we only have to work half a day on Wednesdays.'

Voice: 'What, *every* bloody Wednesday?'

Ah, the wit of the man, the men, the brotherhood. But hey what about the ladies, the sisters in arms?

I've always maintained that the essence of Liverpool wit down the ages had been one part Irish, one part American, and three parts female:

> You can tell a girl who's German
> You can tell a girl who's Swiss
> You can always tell a French girl
> By the way she's learned to Kiss
> You can tell a girl who's Swedish
> You can tell a girl who's Dutch
> You can always tell a Liverpool girl
> But you can't tell her much.

From the earliest days I studied the wit and the wiles of womankind. There are motherly orders that don't make sense:

'Just look at the dirt in your ears!' (Try it.)

There's the twisted logic:

'My real shoe size is four but I'm wearing sevens 'cos fours hurt.'

There's the fatalistic imagery:

'He never takes me anywhere. Me window's me world.'

It took me a complete childhood to realise the awe-inspiring talents of the fairer sex, but you can do it in an afternoon on a self-conducted guided tour of the dockland.

Along that amazing thoroughfare there are numerous cafés (greasy-spoon type) staffed by Liverpool's finest lasses of all sorts and sizes. There's fag-ash Lil who serves every-thing with ash – chips and ash, beans and ash, mash and ash; there's Miss Hygiene who hates smoke and smokers, and Miss Prim who hates foul language and has a swear-box at the ready. Their repartee takes no prisoners:

'Excuse me, love, there's a fly in my cake.'

'Let's have it back and I'll give you a currant.' Or:

'Miss, this steak's funny.'

'Well, laugh at it.'

I used to frequent these places and observe the waitresses in full flow. There is the more than credible tale of an American sailor who was visiting Liverpool for the first time and not having the best of days. Feeling peckish, he enters a dockland café, sits down, ignores the list of food chalked on the wall and shouts out to the waitress:

'I've come all the way from America and I want something special: I'll have a sheep's head.'

The girl opens the swing door to the kitchen and yells: 'Sheep's head one.'

'Hey! I want it done American style.'

'Take the brains out!'

True? If it isn't, it ought to be! Scouse wit is often directed at overweening outsiders. Often it's sharp to the point of cruelty; other times it's gently deflating: Two blokes laying paving stones are being watched by an American tourist, who says: 'What are you guys doing?'

'Flagging, mate. You put your sand down, lay the slab on top and tap it home with this rubber hammer.'

'Gee, that's interesting. But I'm in computer engineering, and I have to work to the nearest thousandth of an inch.'

'That's no good to us, lad – we've got to be spot on.'

See what I mean?

The other side of the coin shows in the story of the young sailor from a visiting Russian destroyer who is waiting at a dock road bus stop clutching a piece of paper.

'Excuse, please,' he says to a passer by, 'I'm a stranger here – I try to find my way. A kind man on docks has write on this paper, what I should ask for. Could you tell me what it says?' The Scouser examines the piece of paper, on which is written: 'Tell him nothing'.

My home town gave me many insights into humour and life in general. It taught me priorities, like the strength of family ties, particularly in severe adversity, and the value of true friends no matter how successful or otherwise one becomes. It taught me simple lessons in the value of money, or the fun of not having it. My town was, and still is, an unending source of material for me.

Five years ago I was home doing a concert and was amazed at the lack of night life 'buzz' compared to the heady days of the '60s, '70s and early '80s. Many thousands of city dwellers had moved out to the satellite towns – Skelmersdale, Kirkby *et al*, and no longer felt the urge to return. How sad, thought I – the good days seemed to be gone for good. Not true.

Two years later I'm home and feel that old familiar thrill of streets busy day and night, heads held high, laughter almost back to the old raucous pitch. Thank God, I thought, the land's back with the people. I put these thoughts to a Liverpool taxi driver, who, as always, conversed out of the side of his mouth and over his shoulder.

'I think the town's come back to life. Don't you?'

'No, mate, this place is still on the deck. I'll tell you how bad things are. It's eight months since anybody's been sick in the back of this car!!'

But I must not be carried away with the 'Pool and lose the thread of my tale. Many a time I will return to quote truth and a little fiction from my past but for now, and to round off this chapter, let me take you through the totally one-off experience of a Liverpool wedding – or the overview of several weddings.

I suppose the change in my cabaret act from gags to routines began with 'The Wedding'. Written and performed nearly 25 years ago, it is still a must when I work to fellow townies.

The basis of the sketch is that weddings in the old days were a heady mixture of romance, family strife and outrageous fun. Five-part weddings we had: church, pub, house, pub, house. Out of the church at ten to three in the afternoon and everyone scrambling to get to the pub before last orders.

'Wait, I must get some shots,' cries the photographer forlornly.

'Take one big picture and cut it up afterwards,' bellows the best man, anxious to get to the bookies before the 3 o'clock race at Thirsk.

Oftentimes the whole entourage, including the bride in her veil, would crash into the local boozer and sink several pints. And there we would find the interloper. He was a cutie. He'd seek out the bride's father and say:

'You don't know me, but I was at the service and I must say she looked beautiful.'

'Thanks, mate. Hey, come on in and join us for a jar.'

That did it. Interloper was well and truly ensconced, drinking free ale, ravaging the buffet and helping to carry beer crates back to the house. Only he never made it to the house, and neither did the beer crates. He was never seen again – but he was in all the wedding photographs!

Back at the house the two families took sides to be seated. The meal was always salad. All the knives and forks had little bits of string on to show who lent them. As soon as somebody dropped a cup they were all down on their knees to see whose it was.

'What are you doing on the corned beef table? You're on the ham table with our family. Their crowd's on the potted meat – move them down!'

'Are you a friend of the groom?'

'Certainly not, I'm the bride's mother.'

After the meal it was back to the pub till closing time – everyone still in wedding attire, which was a little Guinness-smeared by now.

'Are you with the wedding party?'

'Yeah.'

'Do you want to buy a watch?'

'What's it like?'

'Sh! The fellow next to you's wearing it.'

So on to closing time and back to the house for the customary fight.

'When we get back there, keep you gob shut.'

'Why, luv?'

'You know the trouble you caused at Billy's funeral. So no more of it.'

Actually, the trouble would begin in the simplest of ways, with Uncle Harry toasting the happy couple.

'Well, I'd like to wish my favourite nephew all the best in his venture. I think we all know what a fine boy he is and what a family of swines he's married into. He may be able to make an honest girl out of his missus, although lies have been told to get him to the altar.'

'Don't you say a word about that girl,' would come from the bride's mum. 'That girl's my world.'

'Listen, Harry – you button your lip or I'll button it for you.' And suddenly the battle was on. Chairs smashing, heads breaking, noses bleeding, women screaming. Always at the rear of the fracas would be Uncle Jimmy, crying plaintively: 'Mind the ale lads, mind the ale.'

Ten minutes and several blows later the police (or rather a single policeman) would arrive and contemplate the carnage: 'What's the trouble?'

'No trouble here, officer. We were doing the Hokey Cokey and we bumped into each other.'

3

How I ended up at a teacher-training college is still a bit of a mystery. Having decided that a university degree was beyond me, and having had a parental thumbs down to working on the docks, I suppose it was the only option left. Armed with a couple of 'A' levels and a sprint speed of even time for the 100 yards, I left grammar school in 1957 much, I'm sure, to the delight of several members of staff. No, I wasn't a troublesome pupil – just a little mischievous. OK, so I locked young Swindlehirst in the class coke burner; and, yes, I organised a 'dropping time' for class 5A. This involved keeping our eyes on the electric wall clock, which clicked on the minute. On the stroke of 3 pm everybody in the class dropped a ruler, pencil or some such. This turned Mr Preston into a raving lunatic and brought down the wrath of the headmaster on us all. Oh yes, and I suppose it was me who inspired the 'stand up' lessons. Every time the teacher turned to the blackboard we would all stand up and then wait until the last split second to sit down before he turned back to face the class. Good old-fashioned, harmless fun that probably cost me the position of head boy.

But enough of that and on to Simmaries Training College, Strawberry Hill, Twickenham, where my true potential would shine. I loved college, not just for the freedom from home ties, but also for the chance to meet blokes from all walks of life – ex-servicemen, officers and ranks, retired policemen, ex-schoolboys like me. All with talents that I was eager to learn. Typing, languages, guitar playing – even drumming. Yes, I was the college drummer for two years. My drum kit was passed through the back window of the college on many a night after curfew. I learned country guitar and used to perform at college reviews. Later, as social secretary, I even wrote and produced some shows. Great preparation for an, as yet, unthought of leap into showbusiness.

To begin with, college life is nothing if not organised, from the waking up to the crashing out, the whole day is neatly planned. Lectures in the early morning, then lunch, then sport and entertainment for the rest of the day and night. We had several drinking haunts, the most notable being the Waldegrave pub. Here it was that many a student over-imbibed and consequently overslept in the mornings thus missing lectures. Here's where my talents came into their own. It was my responsibility, on mornings after, to attend lectures and answer in several different voices during roll-call. Often I would shout 'here' for more names than were actually present in the whole gathering!

This was the start of my march towards the most coveted job in the college – the position of social secretary. He was the man. He was a law unto himself. The social sec got to organise all the major events from coming up ball to jazz concerts, to revues, to the going down ball. He was the person with his finger on the pulse of the student body. Remember, in those days, Simmaries was an all male institution, so the social secretary was responsible for attracting ladies to its functions.

'Doc' O'Connell was my predecessor. He was also the leader of the country dance band and a fine accordion player. It was 'Doc' who took me under his wing and eventually turned me into a drummer. You see, in my teens, I'd been a fan of Irish dancing and had attended many ceilidh dances. So I knew the jigs and reels and waltzes and their tempos. Hence it was easy to adapt to banging drums in the various rhythms.

So the band and the name answering were two rungs on the ladder to fame, but what of the third and major step?

Well, this came about by placing myself in the centre of the college universe – the snooker room. Here I could meet and natter to all and sundry. Learn a fact here, give a little advice there and generally spread a little jollity with my wisecracks. Uncle Tom's lessons in the art of snooker and billiards came in handy. But I always restrained my impulse to beat everyone out of sight, preferring to heed the words of Rudyard Kipling and 'yet not look too good nor talk too wise'.

All these efforts were rewarded when, in July 1959, I was elected social secretary for the following year – one of the proudest moments of my life – even though I only scraped in by five votes, one of which was mine!

I didn't want to go home for the summer holiday that year in case the dream was broken, and counted the days to my return – September 1958 and the coming up ball at York House, Richmond. I'd booked the hall, the band and organised coaches to transport 140 girls from local colleges, guaranteeing to the various principals that their charges would all return by midnight.

What I didn't account for was the fecklessness of my fellow man. Sure enough, four coaches of ladies arrived at 8 pm but there was not a bloke in sight. All were ensconced in nearby pubs and remained there until 9 pm.

This left Jim Molyneux and me to face the wrath of 100 plus beauties. Jim's a great chap, St Helens born and proud of it, a man you'd stand next to in the jungle or in a fire fight, but not a man to cope with irate womenfolk. So, true to form, Jim beat a hasty retreat leaving T O'C to face the flak.

'You can do it. That's why we voted for you,' was his last word on the subject.

So I was alone, except for a room full of beautiful girls who actually didn't appear to be too upset. Well, all except one, a dark-haired lass wearing (I'll never forget it) green stockings.

'Where's the men? Eh? I've got number one cloakroom ticket and there's not a man here,' shrieked this Yorkshire accent.

'I'm here aren't I?' I mumbled. 'Why don't we lead the floor?'

And we did. This student from Digby Stuart College, Roehampton, led me many a dance both that night and the rest of my life. This was Pat Finan the girl I would marry. The girl I knew I would marry the very moment I met her, even if it was on the wrong end of an ear bashing.

Pat it was who eventually dragged me away from drumming because I was the only one who never got a break on band nights. Pat it was who also convinced me that my athletic days were coming to an end. In an inter-year competition I ran 100 yds, 220 yds and relay, but also had to fill gaps in the pole vault and mile. My future wife refused to appreciate the need to take part, as opposed to winning, and heckled me during my 5 ft pole vault ('I can jump higher meself') and literally handbagged me whilst I slowly jogged for a place in the mile. Still, she is the reason I'm here to write this book. Pat, my family, my friends – oh, and Vin Hadley. Vin was a Norwich lad who was the greatest actor I'd ever seen. He could play any part, particularly comedy. He taught me timing, stage presence, miming (we performed Stan Freberg's 'John and Marsha', with me as the girl!) and the art of choosing which gag to tell at which time.

So after 12 months learning to teach, I was on stage delivering such immortal gems as: 'She's so ugly, when she sucks a lemon the lemon pulls a face,'; and 'He's so thin when he was a kid he won a race he couldn't break the tape, it cut his neck!' and 'He's so unlucky he broke his leg in the eye hospital.'

My big finish used to be the three blokes in uniform chasing the naked beauty. A passer-by says 'What's going on?'

'They're trying to recapture an escapee from the local asylum,' says a local.

'Why is the bloke at the back carrying two buckets of sand?'

'That's his handicap, sir – *he* caught her last week!'

It always got them, that gag; shows you what a lousy sense of humour college folk had in those days. Still, it was all good practice and a lot of fun.

Who'd have thought that three years and two children later I'd be relying on that training to help eke out an inadequate teacher's wage. It seems marriage, or potential marriage, brings out the grafter in people. Even in my last year in college I was saving money to wed Pat as soon as I could. To this end I took to typing out people's theses for a small fee. I taught local children mathematics to 'O' level standard at the rate of 10s per hour. I even worked in a bakery at nights for £12 for a 12-hour shift.

I loved the bakery but couldn't stand the boredom of some of the jobs. I hated having to place glacé cherries in the middle of iced cakes as they rolled past on a conveyor belt. Indeed on my last night I realised a long held dream by slinging a whole bucketful at the belt and leaving two or three cakes pebble-dashed and several score un-cherried. Later, I read of the London bus driver who on his last day before retirement drove round Eros three times before carrying on, and I know just how he felt.

Throughout these days my absorbent brain was soaking up all forms of information. Some via television but more so from radio – or wireless as we knew it. My heroes were the funny men who could encapsulate in a few words a complete domestic situation. A classic example was this one-liner from the great Al Read:

Wife: 'That's an awful lot of aftershave for a darts match.'

The poetry of it, the simplicity of it, and, for me, the lure of it. Where else could one get the thrill of a room full of people laughing? Never mind screaming groupies – give me screams of laughter.

How lucky I would be to meet and often work with my heroes. Arthur Askey, the first star to ever call me mate. How funny he was, how kind, and how truthful.

Once Arthur was touring with a variety show and was asked how it was going. 'Lousy,' said the little man.

'I suppose the press are to blame?'

'No, no,' he replied, 'funny enough, the critics have been very kind. It's word of mouth that's wiping us out!' Nice one Arthur. Pleasure to know you sir – sorry to lose you.

But it's a long way from teaching in Bootle to meeting Arthur Askey in a Royal Variety Show. How do you bridge the gap? Well, you can start by having three kids in three years.

Pat had taught before and after having our first two babies, but on the arrival of Frances, our third, she decided it was too much to ask our mothers to cope with the nappies and noise. Suddenly our family budget went down from £14 per week to £7 and disaster loomed! Enter Eddie Farrell, a school pal and local butcher who had dabbled in the world of pop groups and who had heard of a vacancy for a group at the Selwyn pub in Anfield. Eddie it was who enticed me there to meet Brendan McCormack, a brilliant guitarist who now gives classical recitals on guitar and lute, but who had then just retired from the hurly burly of pop tours and wanted to study at home.

Together, as Tom and Brennie, we went on at the Selwyn and did two hours of country music, with me singing and strumming guitar and Brennie following my finger shapes for the chords and melody. Amazingly, we stormed the place and signed up to do two nights a week for £4. A third of this went to Eddie who became our manager and took us to work in his butcher's van. We were the only act to appear on stage smelling of minced meat and wearing shoes covered in sawdust. But we were a hit in our own little way. We broadened our act to include folk songs, protest songs, parodies and even jokes. We made fun of everything, including Brennie, who never spoke or sang in the act, preferring to stand completely po-faced.

'You want to see him when he's upset.'

'Give him a chance – nature didn't.'

'Can you tell he's been eating ugly pills?'

For some reason audiences liked it. Maybe because we picked on targets other than them. They loved laughing at other people's expense. An invaluable lesson learned early in my career: invent the gags, don't make them racist, or religious or sexual, make them happen to you, or your family or a friend of yours. This was particularly true of football gags, which were rife in the '60s and the most frequent cause of open warfare in many clubs and pubs. I made them about my own team – although not revealing which one!

'We never have trouble on the terraces. It's very hard to fight when you're crying.' 'There were so few at the match last week I had to walk thirty yards for a light.' 'Our floodlit game was so awful a frustrated supporter shouted, "Switch those lights off." "Do you mind," retorted another, "I'm reading!"'

Gradually, through folk clubs, working men's clubs and private functions, the act became virtually all comedy. So much so that Brennie decided there was less and less need for him and preferred to carry on with his classical concerts. This obliged me to do a double act on my own: not easy.

I suppose Wigan was the place that changed my life. Wigan, a great town that entered the twentieth century later than most and bred warm-hearted, although hard to please, audiences:

'Nobody claps us coming out of the pit.'

'What's the comic like?' 'He's all right if you like laughing.'

'He's about as funny as a kick in the groin.'

'Well, at least he didn't disturb the sale of bingo tickets.'

Despite these and similar remarks, Wigan was a good town for me. Newtown British Legion was the first venue at which I went on alone. Frank Law, the compère was really kind and pointed me in the right direction. 'Hello Tom!' [God, he's called me Tom] 'If I was you I'd do all the gags in the first spot. Second half they'll be drunk and you can sing with the guitar.' He was right! Two spots and £10 later I was feeling great. The audience liked me: clean gags, some good country songs, no bad language, and they felt – rightly as it happened – that they had discovered me. What a night! I determined to remember every name from that momentous occasion so I noted them in my diary. Doorman, compère, chairman, concert secretary, paymaster, and all their personal details – name of wife, any particular affliction, favourite drink and so on. Later this ensured a warm return to that and every other club. 'What a nice lad! Even remembered our names. We should have him here more often.'

Wigan taught me many lessons in one night and it started the word of mouth campaign that years later would lead me to the London Palladium. Meantime, it was good to do well in the working men's clubs two – sometimes three times a night. Gradually the act broadened – less jokes as such – more observations and sketches.

'I just met a bloke outside carrying a case of champagne. He said it was a third prize in the club raffle. Second prize was a Jaguar car. First prize was a job on the committee.' Roars from the members, though sometimes the story was too close to home to be funny.

I soon learnt that, when in Wales you don't try to

tell Welsh jokes, or Wigan jokes in Wigan. You're from Liverpool – so you do Scouse jokes. They were new to the audience, and were guaranteed not to upset local feelings.

'Things are so slack on Liverpool's docks, fellers are taking stuff back.'

'Twenty-two dockers were pulling a boat in. The rope snapped and nobody fell over.'

'Me dad used to be on the docks, but he's working now.'

'On the subject of me dad …'. And off I'd go, turning all the humour on to my family – making them and not the Irish or Pakistanis the butt of the gag. And sometimes these family stories were absolutely true. For instance, my mother was a lover of all things religious and when the Pope decided to hold an ecumenical council of all churches, mother decided to copy him. She invited nuns, priests, a rabbi, a Baptist minister and an Anglican vicar to take tea in their little two-up-two-down house and asked me to call round to help entertain. My dad at the time was 21 stone in weight and working hard at the Gladstone Dock. He returned home about ten minutes after the reverends had arrived and I was sent to tell him to go upstairs and dress in his Sunday suit to 'take tea'. Up he went, size twelves crashing. Down he came, resplendent except for a missing collar (he couldn't find a stud).

'Perhaps you'd pour the tea for the reverends, Pat,' said mother.

So out dad went to the little back kitchen, returning with a tray laden with the best china and a huge teapot. Too late my attention was drawn to the wooden draught excluder nailed to the floor in the doorway. Twenty-one stones hit it at a 100 miles an hour and up went dad and down again, together with our best china and tea all over his Sunday suit.

There he lay purple faced and seething with uncontrolled rage. Staring at the gathered faces of the pious and saintly, he eventually managed to mutter through clenched teeth: 'How very unfortunate.' I was reduced to tears. But I remembered that event and used it everywhere – to the delight of many, including dad.

I relied greatly on family and friends for my source material. I soon abandoned the set-piece joke and developed groups of one-liners that could be built into a sequence:

'My brother's wife is not pretty. Teeth like the Ten Commandments – all broken. She only needs a white one for a snooker set. Big woman: doesn't wear a cross-your-heart bra – she wears a cross-the-street hammock. Mind you, she's good to the kids. She had her ears pierced so they can watch the telly.'

So gradually a jokeless act was forming. It was based on several precepts. Long jokes meant sudden death if the audience knew the gag. One liners didn't count because in a battery of several dozen you were sure to get everyone going with at least half. Patter routines worked best in clubs where the art of the job was to do well in the first spot so that they didn't pay you off at half time. Second spot you could always sing. Believe me, it wasn't easy working to crowds who'd had Dave Allen last night, Ken Dodd the night before, Bob Monkhouse last week.

Red House working men's club Sunderland was a case in point. I went on at noon on a Monday. It was full (when did these guys work?). 'We've had 'em all here, pal, and they've all died a death,' said the secretary with grim satisfaction. He was right – the dressing room walls were full of epitaphs. 'Never again!' 'Abandon hope' – and to make matters worse they were signed by the actual comics. To make the worse worst, all the members knew my fee because the contract was pinned on the club notice board! (This happened in virtually every club in those days.)

So – Stag audience, clean comic whose fee they know – what to do? Football and docks routines – not blue but a little clever.

Liverpool had beaten Newcastle 6–2 on the Saturday, Tony Hateley scoring four goals, so I opened the act by singing: 'Have I told you Hateley that I love you.'

Cheers from the massed Sunderland ranks. The ice was broken. I followed this up with my docks routine and my first spot passed without riot or injury.

'You were lucky, mate,' said the concert secretary. 'If I was you I'd sing in the second half.'

'You're reading my mind, pal,' thought I.

A lucky escape in that club, but not in all. It's said that you've got to die on your feet to strengthen the will to perform – and I got plenty of practice in the art of demise.

'Hope you've enjoyed the meal – the chef's got over his rash.' Silence. 'Great kitchen – one million flies can't be wrong.' Heated mumblings. This was yours truly trying to get a laugh with Mr Flippant Gear in a Manchester night club. Well, how was I supposed to know that three days before there'd been an outbreak of food poisoning in the venue? Exit unpaid comic – closely followed by audience – followed by police. I shook them off at the East Lancashire road. 'Never again,' said my pounding brain. 'No matter how well it appears to work for others – never again for you.'

Or sometimes you just get away with it by the skin of your teeth – as with my lunchtime stint at Bedlinog, a sleepy town in the Aberdare valley. Take hard-working miners, farmers and such, add some pints of beer and you have a room ready for fun, right? Maybe yes, maybe no. Like most other audiences at Sunday lunch shows they'd heard every joke and comic song – they'd got to the stage of mouthing the punch lines. So what to do? To make matters worse, I had to listen to the concert secretary:

'If they don't like you they'll turn their backs and read the Sunday papers. And if they *really* don't like you they'll flick nuts over their shoulders at the stage.'

I thought the only thing to do was to take the mickey. 'I've got to go well today because there's no nuts behind the bar – only in the audience.' (Smiles.) 'I may not be as interesting as the papers but I tell more truths.' (Loud smiles.) 'I know – nobody claps you coming out of the pit.' (Applause. Tom, you're in!) So then the docker's routine, some football gags – a song and off while I still had my health.

'We'll have you back,' said the chairman.

'That's what you think,' thought the comic.

Jimmy Marshall, a great comic of the old school, was not so lucky when he tried his luck at Bedlinog. Mind you, it could be argued that he was a mite short on tact. He opened with the stirring declaration: 'Anyone who flicks nuts at me gets a smack in the gob!' Bingo! – the place erupted, and Jimmy dashed off stage, into his dressing room and threw his suit bag out of the window that was left permanently open against just such little difficulties of this kind. He followed his bag and, hanging from the window sill, was just about to drop to the ground when his ankles were seized from below.

'Gotcha,' cried the local bobby. 'There's been too much thieving from this club.'

'But, but, but . . .' Jim cried in vain as he was frogmarched through the front door.

'Does anyone know this guy?' As one, the baying crowd answered: 'Too bloody right we do – let me at him!!'

Same club – different result. You win some – you lose some.

Look at Pat Mooney. A Liverpool-based Irishman, Pat is extremely funny in a natural sort of way – the breezy archetype of the emigré son of the emerald isle. He enters the fray suited in bright, bright green jacket and pants, often clutching a shelelagh (I'm not sure that doesn't sometimes provoke reaction of the wrong sort) and weighing in at something like 220 pounds.

'What do you think of the suit?' he'll say. 'I leaned over in the dressing room and two blokes started playing snooker on me back.'

Gentle humour, gentle man, and honest with it: 'I didn't die on me feet last night, but I was critically ill.'

Pat is the butt of a classic club tale, told with rueful relish by himself, which offers a warning to comics everywhere. In the 1970s and '80s, one of the most popular home-grown gagsters in the north east of England was a man called Bobby Knoxall, a man for whom I have the greatest respect, more of which I'll tell later. The man was idolised by his fans and was used as a yardstick by concert secretaries in that area. So picture Pat Mooney's debut in a Newcastle working men's club and a typical Geordie introduction:

'Who's the greatest comic you've ever seen?'

'Bobby Knoxall!'

'How much do we pay Bobby Knoxall?'

'Twenty-five pounds.'

'Well, this feller must be good – he's on thirty: Pat Mooney!'

As they say in the business, 'Follow *that* with your sea lions!' Well, Pat tried, but slowly died, to the point that disgruntled mumblings became verbal abuse, and then turned physical: a drunk in the audience picked up a glass ashtray and threw it at the stage. Pat picked it up and hurled it back in the direction from which it came. Unfortunately his aim was slightly off and he hit an old lady a glancing blow. This was enough to incense the male members, who charged the stage. Pat dashed off and barricaded himself in the dressing room.

'Come out you **** so-and-so. We're going to kill you.' (Now, seriously, would you go out?)

'I'm not coming out till the police arrive,' screamed Pat.

'Come on out – we're going to tear you limb from limb.' (I ask you – would you go out?)

'I'm not coming out till the police arrive.'

The pounding and the shouting carried on for about twenty minutes, gradually subsiding when the bingo (top of the bill) started. Minutes later there was a slightly quieter knock on the door.

'Pat, come out,' said the concert secretary.

'No!' affirmed Pat.

'But it's time for your second spot!' said the con sec.

Geordie logic, clubland priority. Poor Pat! Like him, I've served my time in the north east and, like many others, I've learned to love that area, its people and their sense of humour. Let me tell a story that I would be proud to claim as my own but in fact happened to Roy Castle.

Roy was working a social club in Newcastle and wanted to tell the audience of an experience he'd had at the Savoy Grill, but he suddenly realised they might not know where that was, so he said:

'The other week I was in the Savoy Grill. For those who don't know, that's in London.'

A voice on Roy's right boomed: 'Where's London?' 'Well,' said Roy, 'It's south of Sunderland, I'll tell you that.'

'Where's Sunderland?' came a voice from Roy's left.

'Second from bottom!' boomed the man on the right.

Great humour the Geordies. Great comics too. I mentioned Bobby Knoxall earlier. He's an extremely funny and original entertainer. At one time he opened his act to the strains of Matt Munro's hit, 'From Russia with Love', and as he reached the line 'I fly to you', he would dive into the audience, landing on a table and scattering booze and ash trays in all directions. Nobody slept in Bobby's act!

About that time I was scratching a pittance of a living in the working men's clubs of South Wales, an area renowned for great audiences and extremely dodgy agents and concert secretaries (the people who book the acts). I'd given up teaching for a short spell in 1968 and was trying to make the big time but failing miserably. The path I trod sloped ever more steeply downward until I was reduced to driving from Liverpool (pre-motorway) to Cardiff for one night's work and risking not being put on when I arrived. You see, it was a time when agents would book about six acts in a club, let them all do one spot and then sack the three worst with no fees. A cruel sport.

Most comics were aware of this and always checked beforehand:

'Do I get all my fee no matter what?'

If the answer was no, or even a definite maybe, the best course of action was out of the door. 'My name's John and I've gone!'

On one particular Saturday night, finding my last 10s wearing a hole in my pocket, I arrived at a British Legion club and realised I was but one of seven acts and decided to challenge the concert secretary. He hummed and hah-ed but wouldn't say yes to the fee because (I was told by a member) he'd double booked comics and was looking for a way to sack me for nothing. Into the middle of this wrangle strode Bobby Knoxall.

'Got kids, Scouse?' he asked me.

'Three, mate,' said I.

'Worked this week, have you?'

'Not once, Bobby.'

'That does it then. I've had two nights' work and you need this job much more than me. Listen, Taffy,' he said to the concert secretary, 'Put the boy on 'cos I'm leaving and you're not going to get another comic tonight.' And they did put me on, and I did well. Thanks, Bobby, I'll never forget your kindness – and, boy, did I need that eight quid.

When club comedians part they don't say goodbye but, 'Down the road' – a hope that that's where we'll meet again. And down the road is the end of the rainbow, the final resting place, the land of the perfect audience. Down the road can be hard to find, though, particularly if you have to ask your way because for some reason people in Britain can't direct you. Struggling to find a venue in Wrexham, I enquired of a very obvious local, 'Where's the British Legion

Club?' and he directed me as follows: 'Go down here and turn left where the chippy used to be!'

And do you know what? I set off! I even thanked the man!

Worse was to happen when I was booked at the Gracie Fields Theatre in Rochdale. As a memorial to the lovely lady it's a splendid venue – but extremely difficult to find. It was on a wet Rochdale Sunday evening that I called to a passer-by from my car window: 'Excuse me, do you know where the Gracie Fields Theatre is?'

'I'm not right sure,' was the reply, 'but go down to the cemetery and ask someone there!' (I learned later that The Cemetery is the name of a pub; what's more it's situated in – wait for it! – Bury Road.)

We've all probably got a 'getting lost' tale to tell, but one of the best featured the great Irish warbler Ronnie Carroll. Ronnie had been engaged to sing at the Queen's Hotel 'near Glasgow'. Now there's a broad description. Let's face it, in global terms Stockholm is 'near' Glasgow. His general instruction was to leave the city by the Edinburgh Road, and after about six miles to ask one of the locals.

Two miles out of the city Ronnie hailed a passer-by and asked about the Queen's Hotel. The man got into the car saying, 'I'm going that way – I'll show ye.' Off they sped and eight miles further on Ronnie, now a little bothered, asked: 'Is this still the way to the Queen's Hotel?'

'Listen pal, don't worry. I'm taking you to a much better place!'

Ah, the Scots! Can nothing faze them? Consider the salutary experience of Barry Mason, songwriter extra-ordinaire. He's penned some massive hits, none bigger than 'Delilah'. At the height of Tom Jones' popularity, with his version of 'Delilah' at number three in Britain and number one in America, Barry Mason was in an open-topped car at traffic lights in Sauchihall Street. Leaning on the traffic light pole was a Saturday drunk with a bag of fish and a half bottle of Scotch. The man was whistling 'Delilah'.

'Hey, I wrote that,' said Barry.

'Wha?' enquired the drunk.

'That song, "Delilah" – I wrote that.'

'You didna! I've got the record. Les Reed wrote it.'

'Ay yes, but I wrote the words,' said Barry.

'I wasn't whistling the words,' said Mr Glasgow.

There must be hope for a nation that breeds people who, though virtually paralytic with the local cordial, can come out with lines like that.

4

Being a club entertainer is being a person of many parts and it involves highs and lows, goods and bads, great times and 'never agains'. I suppose the best analogy is with the old docks system, where men were sent to jobs and had no idea what was expected of them when they arrived. They could be working with flour, coal, machinery, cranes or even just be book keepers – it all depended on the boss man.

So too in showbusiness at grassroots level. Details of jobs were sketchy. You would arrive at 7.30 pm and ask for the concert secretary, or the pub manager, or just 'Charlie'. Whoever was the boss had complete control of your destiny for the next four hours – and sometimes for years longer! If you were a goodish act and behaved yourself, not only did you get all your fee but you were asked back and even recommended to other clubs on the circuit.

Generally, acts were booked by the yard. Two, three and sometimes four or five half-hour shows were demanded of you, although two was the norm. All right for a singer, or even for a patter man with plenty of patter and a guitar. But what about speciality acts? What about jugglers? How long can people watch balls, clubs and objets-d'art being flung about? And worse than jugglers, what about tumblers – the 'ooh-yaas' (every time one did an athletic flip, the other would shout 'ooh-yaa'). How long could they keep chucking themselves round? Never mind the patience of the audience, what about the sheer physical exhaustion involved? In answer to these questions there is a lovely story of a tumbling act called Flip and Flop who arrived at a working men's club and were told they only had one show to do but it would be half an hour.

'Impossible,' said Flip. 'We only do six minutes.'

'Half an hour,' repeated the con sec.

'Look,' explained Flop, 'we'd love to do half an hour, but we literally, physically can only do six minutes – I mean, that's the limit.'

'Half an hour or you don't get your money, pal!'

'Very well,' sighed Flip. 'We'll do half an hour, but there'll be a lot of walking about.'

Anyway, let me show you clubland through the eyes of the performer, from the sharp end of the spotlights, where nothing that glitters is even silver, never mind gold. As a general rule, club shows in the boom days were presented in time-honoured order: girl singer, comic or specialty act (Flip and Flop), and pop group for dancing to finish the evening. It was sensible planning if you were the paying customer, but a pain in the butt if you were the group. If the latter, you had two choices: either arrive hours early to set up the equipment and then hang around a loo-less dressing room all night; or risk arriving with the others and hope for a bingo break in proceedings to enable you to set up. Whatever the pre-show planning, the acts would always end up crammed backstage in the most primitive of conditions, trying to make the best of it and the idiosyncrasies of the club committee.

I remember once being sent to Rotherham to do a show for £12 and I was told by the agent to give the concert secretary £1 as a sweetener to keep him re-booking. 'Don't worry,' said Len, the agent. 'It'll come out of your commission – just give me the balance of four shillings.'

On the night the con sec, ensuring we were alone, insisted

on £3. 'Get lost,' said I, or words to that effect. 'Now you're getting nothing.'

'Me and my mates are going to sort you out in the car park.'

'OK,' I thought, 'If I'm going down, I'm going down in flames.'

With great relish I opened the bingo machine and pinched a ball. To confuse the committee, I took the fuse out of the bingo machine plug. By the time they found that out, there'd be no time to check the board before the game. Imagine the consternation of the members when the jackpot round had been played and the board was checked and there was a number missing. Terrific!

Devilment in my heart but an angel on my shoulder that night, because when I opened the dressing room window and shimmied outside there was no one about. I'd cadged the use of the group's amplifier for my guitar. The con sec thought it was mine and was waiting for me to pack it up.

I fled from Yorkshire with bingo ball 67 and £12. The money's gone – but the ball's in my snooker room on a plinth.

There were good times aplenty in those days, and every 'turn' had a new club story to tell. There's the classic of the opening of a new venue and the committee agreeing to a no-expenses-spared do. 'Let's get some big names and have a bit of a thrash'.

Come the night, come the funnies. The first act to arrive is the juggler, who senses a storming evening and hopes to get a late-ish time slot after the early jollies and the hour's free booze.

'Who else is on the bill tonight?' he enquires.

'A girl singer and a group.'

'Well,' says the ever hopeful speciality act, 'Why don't you put the girl on first to get them sitting down, then bring on the group to jolly them up, and then hit them with me?'

'Terrific!' says the club secretary. 'So it'll be Shirley Bassey, The Beatles and then Jimmy Hargreaves!'

I remember working the Manchester nightclub circuit. There were some great venues: the Palace, Offerton Palace, Southern Sporting (often referred to as Mafeking) and many more. I'll always remember the first night I arrived for a band call and watched the bar staff pulling literally hundreds of half pints of mild or bitter into pint pots. The doors would open on the dot of eight and people would pile in and rush to beat everyone else to the bar. If only they'd known how flat their first drink was going to be.

In those days it was possible to work three or even four clubs in one evening, doing the same half-hour spot and using taxis to get from one venue to the next. One night I shared the cab with a stripper, who followed me on at each venue and then raced out, clad only in a fur coat, and proceeded to dress in the back of the cab as we drove to the next club.

Unsure of my chat when away from my Liverpool audiences, I used to do a short comedy-magic routine to pad out my act, and relied on a lucky choice of female volunteer from the audience. One of Murphy's laws states that when everything is going well you don't need all the ammunition, but when things are going badly all your bullets are blanks. I had a clear case of that in the last club of my run one night. Having been taxied to the rear of three clubs, I began to believe they could all be the same one and that I was in a time warp. On stage at the fourth, things started to unravel. After four gags, no laughter. After four minutes, not a monkeys. What was wrong? Had they heard *all* the jokes? Were they just drunk and incapable of laughing? Did they hate me because I was a Scouser cast adrift in Manchester?

In desperation I clicked into the magic routine and selected a blonde girl near the back who was wearing the shortest mini skirt I'd ever seen. Would she help me? No chance!

Please? Never! (Come on, love, you'd be helping to get a desperate comic off the hook.) Eventually after pleas, sobs, promises of many drinks and virtually the deeds of my house, the lady acceded to my request and stood up. Too late! My God, too late! No wonder she wanted to stay where she was. If I say she was $8\frac{1}{2}$ months pregnant I am erring on the early side. No wonder her skirt had ridden up to her bottom. Wait a minute – there's worse: the lady was German, could speak hardly a word of English and to compound the problem she was married to the drummer!

So, no comic chat because of the language barrier. No jollies about the look of her figure or legs, and no sympathy for the magic trick.

'Phoney!'

'Fiddle!'

'Set it up with the drummer!'

'Gerroff!'

Which is what I did without delay. I collected my half fee and fled to the taxi.

'I'll never work here again,' I said to the doorman.

'How did you know that?' he replied.

Comedians love to relate the deaths they have died on stage. We seem to wear our wounds with pride, like battle honours that only the good can bandy about. Perhaps singers don't suffer the same way – although my friend Tony Christie can tell many a tale against himself. At one particular venue Tony realised early on that the organist was terrible. No timing, couldn't read music, didn't know any topical songs. He couldn't even anticipate or 'vamp till ready'. The only thing to do was struggle on and rely on Mel James (Tony's guitarist) to cover the cracks. But what about future singers? Tony decided to help his fellow performers by explaining the shortcomings of the organist to the club chairman. Perhaps the committee were not aware of the situation. As he was being paid (rule number 1: always get your money before lodging a complaint), Tony was about to speak his mind when the organist walked past the dressing room and called:

'Cheerio, then! See you again maybe.'

'Oh, he's not your regular organist,' said Tony.

'Wish he was, mate. Wish he was,' said the chairman.

But back to the comics. Consider the case of Johnny Hammond, who claims with some justice to be the unluckiest guy in the business. Everything seems to happen to this gentle, talented son of the north-east. Take the Sunday dinner show he allowed himself to be conned into doing. A late riser on the Sabbath, Johnny was enjoying a mid-day cuppa when the phone rang. It was the secretary of the local working men's club.

'Fancy making fifteen quid?'

'Sure! When?'

'In 15 minutes!'

'Bit short notice, isn't it? Someone let you down?'

'You *could* say that. Get down here and I'll explain things.'

Out strode our comic, suit bag on shoulder and marched the hundred or so yards to the club. On his arrival he was greeted by a flotilla of police cars, formed in a half circle around the club door, blue lights flicking but no sirens. In fact, no noise at all. Police in various outfits were positioned around the building but, thinking it none of his particular business, Johnny ignored it all and went inside. In the foyer he was greeted by a stand-up row between the concert secretary and the (fully clothed) stripper.

'If you think I'm going on that stage you're seriously mistaken.'

'Come on, love, do us a favour.'

'Not on your bloody life.'

'What's going on, Jim?' enquired Johnny.

It turned out that thirty minutes earlier a local man had had a brainstorm after a family row. He'd grabbed a .38 revolver and shot his father-in-law in the head, killing him instantly. The killer had bounded out of the house and into the packed club, taking over a chair at the front and scattering onlookers as he placed the gun on the table in front of him. Two plain-clothes policemen, disguised as waiters, were waiting to pounce, but needed some kind of distraction to trigger off the action. The stripper decided to give it a miss in case her particular assets were not to the gunman's taste.

This was not Johnny's thinking. He thought positive, as do all comedians. If, just if, Johnny could distract the man and save the day, goodness knows what good publicity it would accrue. So on stage went our would-be hero, ignoring the first rule of showbusiness: 'Think before you act.'

Hammer, hammer, hammer went the gags and down down down they sank – falling like dead leaves in front of an audience too horror and panicstricken to react. In fact the only person who was thoroughly enjoying the show was the gunman. He was loving every minute, chortling with glee at every line. Luckily, he was so enthralled that the police were able to pounce and disarm him.

As the long arm of the law was dragging him handcuffed to the door Johnny cried plaintively: 'No, no. Not him! He's all right. It's these other buggers you want to throw out.'

Everything happens to Johnny. Well, it happens to every comic, and probably to singers as well. But comics wear their disasters with pride. Mickey Walker is one who can tell of a crisis or two, but he does it so well it's funnier than most people's acts. Mickey is a bluff, jovial character – an ex-roadie for Elton John, a fine musician and extremely funny in a loud way. He featured prominently in a comedy series I fronted for BBC TV, and was the most riotous warm-up man we ever had. But the best of Mickey belongs to a rainy November night in a Solihull Workies' club.

Booked to do two spots, Mickey went on at 8.30 pm. He hit them with everything – and might as well have been talking to the wall. The concert room was full of noise, bingo sellers, arguments over the day's football and raucous laughter from a crowded bar. Twenty-five minutes of fine comedy was greeted with very little and our hero retired, extremely hurt, to the safety of the dressing room and the comfort of his wife's sympathy.

'What a shower!' he fumed. 'My worst crowd ever – they just didn't want to know. But I bet they keep quiet enough for the bingo.' And suddenly a mad, wonderful idea stole into his mind. 'They've wrecked my act – so I'll wreck their bingo.'

Around the dressing room were strewn various remnants of some past celebration: semi-deflated balloons, streamers, kazoo-type blowers, and other manifestations of noisy fun. 'Why don't I strip down to my Union Jack underpants, festoon myself with streamers and stamp across the stage blowing a kazoo just at the moment when the bingo starts. Yes, that'll teach them!'

So, patiently, the bold Mickey Walker waited his time. Eventually through the thin dressing-room wall came the sound of silence and then the unrecognisable mumblings of a compère through a crackly loudspeaker. This was his moment, and out stepped the jubilant comic – streamer-bedecked, stripped to his Union Jack underpants, and blowing 'The Saints Go Marching In' on a kazoo.

Dear God – what was this? Too late, Mickey realised that the whole audience had risen to its feet, not to welcome his entrance but as a sign of respect for the chairman who (it turned out) had died that afternoon, and for whom the compère had called for two minutes' silence. What to do? What to do? Leave it to a comic to do the only thing possible. Mickey carried on marching and blowing and made his way through a stunned club, out into the street, round to the car park, and an extremely hasty retreat, leaving behind several props, his music and, of course, his fee.

Worse things can happen to a comic – like, for instance, coming second in a contest with a heckler. I've learnt by experience never to take on a heckler if I can possibly avoid it. Others, however, can't resist the challenge. One such is Dave Evans – zany comedian, brilliant impressionist and fine musician and singer. Dave was working the summer season with me at Paignton and was doing Sunday concerts at various holiday camps along the south coast. At one particular venue he was due to follow a girl singer and decided to have a sneak look at the audience through a slit in the curtains. At the front table sat a family of contrasts. Mum had rollers in her hair, a jumper with sleeves rolled up to reveal tattoos, and no teeth. The four children were straggle haired and shod in plastic sandals. Dad, however, was resplendent in white dinner jacket and trousers, white wing-collared shirt and white bow tie. He yelled to the barman in a coarse Cockney accent:

'Yes, two bottles of champagne, that's for this table. Yeah, over here mate.' Then, to the surrounding tables:

'Anyone care to join us in a glass of bubbly?'

Meantime the girl singer had finished and was replaced by Dave Evans, entering more or less to the sound of his own feet and plunging straight into some well-tried patter. Three gags in he was surprised to hear the voice of the punter in the dinner jacket enquiring loudly, of no-one in particular:

'Is this fellow funny? Is it just me or does anyone else think he's awful? I mean, would you say he was funny?'

'Excuse me, Champagne Charlie,' said Dave. 'Do you really want me to be funny?'

'Yes.'

'Well, lend me your suit.'

Gales of laughter from the audience, even some applause, a look of hatred from the front table – but Dave was up and running, with the audience on his side.

On leaving to a standing ovation, Dave returned to the dressing room. A few seconds later the door nearly came off its hinges as Champagne Charlie burst in, red in face, screaming hysterically and looking for revenge. Spotting a lady in the corner of the room he let rip with some foul language on the subject of her features and her taste in clothes. The lady burst into tears and ran out of the room. 'What do you think of that, matey?' asked Champagne Charlie.

'Don't worry me pal – she's not my wife!' said Dave.

Indeed not – she was married to a 6 ft 2 in bass player who stormed in and belted the punter in the nose, leaving him hurt both physically and psychologically, and Dave ecstatic in the belief that, after all, there was a God!

Of course, most audiences aren't as biliously aggressive as this cockney. None the less, the public can be decidedly idiosyncratic in their response to actors in general – witness the following couple of true stories.

Harry Lock is a fine actor and has appeared in countless films going back over many years. He has one of those faces which is instantly recognisable but which is not always easy to put a name to. Like all entertainers, of course, he's always delighted when people not only remember his name but recall even his minor film appearances. So here we have Harry walking to the shops and being overhauled by a gentleman in his sixties.

'Excuse me, but you're Harry Lock aren't you? – The actor, I mean.'

'That's right.'

'In 1957 you appeared in a film called *The Red Beret* with Alan Ladd.'

'I did.'

'You played a sergeant-major in the paratroopers, didn't you?'

'Correct again.'

'You were killed very early in the film weren't you?'

'I was.'

'Would you like to know what happened after you died?'

You can't write stories like that, or like this one involving

Noël Coward. Apparently Coward had gone to Brighton to visit a theatre where one of his epics was opening. The show was a sell-out and he wanted to go backstage to wish the cast well. Not knowing the theatre layout, he approached the grumpy old lady in the box office.

'Before you start – we're full,' she snapped. 'Not a seat. Come back tomorrow.'

'You don't understand, my dear lady. I merely want to find the stage door.'

'Full, I tell you – not a seat!'

'Madame, I do *not* wish to *see* the show. Do you understand. I know all about the show, my dear. You see, I wrote it. I wrote the words and I wrote the music.'

'Oh, yes,' she sniffed. 'A proper little Ivor Novello aren't we?'

Ah. The public. The man, and woman, in the street. They make us what we are. They keep us sane and level headed. They are funnier than even they know. For me, if they want to heckle, let them. For me, if they want to make additions to my act, let them. Believe me, in the long run, it's better all round to bow the knee rather than take them on.

Let me explain why.

5

The first time I noticed the humour of an audience was from the safety of backstage, watching a comedian dying on his feet. As a guitar-vocalist I had opened the bill in a Glasgow pub and appeared to have pleased the clientele. On bounced the comic – Joe King, believe it or not – and he battered away with some tried and trusted material. Result – nothing, zilch, big fat zero. Silence. On and on he hammered, patter, patter. Nothing. No noise, no laughter, no movement. Except, that is, for a large chap right in the front who was scribbling with pencil on paper.

'Are you writing these jokes down?' asked Joe.

'I'm ticking them off!' came the reply.

Never disturb a quiet audience or you'll be sorry.

I told that story to Rolf Harris. He didn't laugh but smiled ruefully and admitted to a similar experience. Rolf was playing at a miners' welfare club in Barnsley. It was a Sunday night, Rolf was riding his success with 'Tie me kangaroo down, sport', and the show was a sell-out.

Arriving in the car park, Rolf was met by the concert secretary with a word of caution.

'The club heckler's in, Mr Harris, and he's lethal. Don't upset him, please.'

'Club heckler? What does he do for a living?'

'He's a miner.'

'That all? And I'm supposed to be afraid of him? Look, friend, I've had years of experience of dealing with people like – what's his name?'

'Albert.'

'Albert. Just you leave him to me and see how a heckler is put down.'

So the buzz went round the club: 'Rolf Harris's taking on Albert.' A bit like a gunfight. No – *very* like a gunfight.

'Good evening, ladies and gentleman.'

'Get off, you're rubbish.'

'Albert, stand against the wall, that's plastered as well.'

'Ha, ha! Get off – you're rubbish.' Albert was nothing if not single-minded.

'Put your hat on, there's a woodpecker in the room.'

'Funny – Fun-nee. Get off, you're rubbish!'

Rolf decided it was time for dirty tricks: 'Look, Albert, you're very funny – almost as funny as when you were making the date with the fellow in the gents earlier on.'

'Are you calling the date off?' enquired Albert.

What a cracking line. It floored Rolf, as it would have floored any comic. So be careful when on stage. Unless it's vital – don't mess with hecklers.

Over the years I've been lucky and double lucky. God alone knows what could have happened to me if the angel on my shoulder had blinked for a split second. Consider my first ever nightclub job. I won't tell you where it was, except to say Lancashire. My agent had talked me into doing four nights at a late-night drinking club. (I was still teaching at school during the day.) The late nights and early mornings were surprisingly easy to cope with. The audiences weren't.

The club stage was only about nine inches off the floor and on crowded evenings it was not unknown for punters to walk across the stage, ignoring the performer, in order to get to the bar. Noise was always ringing round the room – mostly coming from the gambling tables. This was before the days of the breathalyser, and most of the audience would be smashed out of their skulls and ripe for the old drunk gag routines:

'Six of us in the car. We had to let Charlie drive – he was too drunk to sing.'

'They took a sample of his blood and gave it back to him in a glass with an olive in it.'

'He blew up the bag and two days later the Russians shot it down over Siberia. The policeman was still hanging to it. Singing, Nellie Dean.'

They liked the one liners, so that's what I gave them. That and many country songs that they could sing, or sway to, or even dance to on stage with me. Anything for a quiet life, and an easy night. I could live with that – but not so the top of the bill. He was a tenor, semi-operatic whatever that meant, a man of years of experience of theatres, but a man who couldn't live with a room full of bustle and noise while he was singing. Each night he complained to the management. Each night they promised changes. Each night it was the same again. Towards the weekend it got worse, and fights started breaking out. There were rumours of serious trouble over gambling. It came to a head on the Saturday, luckily ten minutes after I'd come off.

As my forty pounds were being counted into my hand in ones, I heard the tenor berating a member of the audience.

'Oh yes – fall asleep while I'm in the middle of a song. Good God – you'd think he could at least sit straight until I finish.'

In fact, it wasn't a question of manners. The man had been stabbed to death through the back of the chair, the victim of some local gang war.

'Sorry about that, son. But we'll make it up to you. We'll have you back,' promised the manager.

'By hell you won't,' said I, and they never did!

But there were always delightful incidents and people to keep me going in the early days. Harry Hoare, for instance. Harry attempted to do a magic act in working men's clubs.

He did card tricks, and the hankies, and swords. But, for me, his forte was pigeons – not because he was any good with them but because of his method of acquiring them. Not for Harry the bother of breeding the creatures and training them for years. Oh, no – he just went out and kidnapped a few from the sea front at Liverpool. Armed with pockets full of bird seed, Harry would plonk himself down on a bench at the Pier Head and throw handfuls to the pigeons, gradually drawing them nearer and nearer until he could grab one and ram it into his pocket. And he had pockets like a poacher. Enough to hold half a dozen birds.

So on the night of each performance Harry would be kitted out with a suit full of wild pigeons – or 'mickeys', as he called them. To be fair they did at least remain in their pockets until they were produced on stage, but once out in the open they would fly into the rafters of the club and relieve themselves on the audience – a practice that began to lose its novelty value after about a minute and a half. You could always tell a club where Harry was on the bill: it had to stay open an extra hour to allow him to entice the birds down with a jar of seed.

I loved Harry, and so did the audiences. But then audiences are strange folk. I'd love to know what goes on in their collective minds.

Another vivid memory from my earliest days concerns the Embassy Club, which was situated above a block of shops opposite Liverpool abattoir. The club was a night spot that had gambling, cabaret and, most importantly, a late bar (2 am as I recall). It was 1965, I was working full time as a teacher, and was in the running for the deputy headship of our school. There was a nun and me neck and neck. At night I was playing the guitar and earning more per week than teaching paid in a month.

One Saturday night at the Embassy we had a packed house. As a rule audiences look the same to me from the stage. On this occasion my short-sightedness did not allow me to see that the men were well over 40 years of age and the women well under 25. It was a bouncy kind of night. The compère had livened up the house, the girl singer had stormed the place and I was going well. That is, until the doors burst open and every policeman in Liverpool rushed into the place. As whistles blew and people ducked for cover, my only thought was 'The nun has got the job. The nun has got the job.'

The inspector leaped on to the stage and I backed off in the direction of the bass player.

'Don't worry, Tommy,' he whispered, 'You're a bona fide visitor. Your name's in chalk on the wall. Sit here with me.'

So there we sat on the bass amplifier while the inspector said through the mike:

'This is a raid. I repeat, this is a raid. Bring me the membership book.'

The book, which must be signed by all the punters, was produced and the inspector leafed through to the day's date. After a minute he said:

'Will the following people please stand up: Mickey Mouse, George Washington, Horatio Nelson....'

As the room chortled with glee, my gaze fell on a docker who was quietly drinking a pint of mild. A bobby came up, grasped the hand containing the glass and said sternly: 'Don't drink that pint – it's evidence.'

The docker obediently put down the pint – and immediately ordered another from the barman! It goes to show something, though I'm not quite sure what.

One of the reasons why I try to swerve away from direct audience participation is because it's so difficult to predict the responses of individual punters. I learned this lesson very early on in my showbiz career. My big chance had come because the local nightclub, Allinson's, in Litherland – had engaged me for a whole week. A dream come true! I'd been lucky enough to get tickets for Pat and me to see shows there. The Drifters, Long John Baldry, Adam Faith had all appeared at Allinson's, and now it was my turn. Not only was I going to appear, I was going to earn £70 for the week. Wow!

But wait a moment. What to do? What sort of act would best suit the club's audience? After all, I was acutely conscious that I was still serving my comic's apprenticeship, and I welcomed all the advice I could get. It never occurred to me that the act I had was the reason I'd been engaged. Booked as known: perform as known. But, no, I had other ideas and I went out of my way to ask regular members of the club what sort of act the audiences liked best.

'A sure winner is getting people to come up on stage,' enthused one. 'Gerry and the Pacemakers got a crowd up there doing "Old Macdonald had a farm" and stuff like that.'

So that was it eh! Use the crowd. But how? I thought back to my college days and tried to remember a routine we did one rag day. Yes, that was it – the whistle routine! That was the answer, I was sure. But I would need to rehearse it first. It so happened that the week before Allinson's I was booked at the Strand club, a small but friendly nightspot near my house that was frequented by many friends, schoolmates and ex-pupils of mine: the ideal place and occasion to try out my pièce-de-résistance:

'Could I have a volunteer? Perhaps the lady in the short black dress? Yes, you love. Would you help me on stage? I won't hurt you unless you ask!'

My volunteer was only too delighted to oblige, and I launched into the spiel. I handed her a referee's whistle and asked her to blow it. She duly gave a couple of blasts to prove how loud it was. I took the whistle from her while I explained what were were going to do.

'I'm going to guess things about you,' I said. 'If I guess wrongly, blow the whistle as loudly as you can.' She nodded, and I handed her the whistle. Well, to be strictly accurate, it was not *the* whistle but another, identical in appearance but with the pea removed and with a blocked-up mouth-piece.

'The price of your dress,' I said. 'Two pounds?' Loud puffs on the whistle but no noise.

'Correct!' said I to roars from the audience.

'And your age,' I continued. 'Fifty-one!' More silent puffs.

'Two out of two!' the punters roared again.

The whole thing went off beautifully, and after my spot I decided to reward my lady volunteer with a large drink. Approaching her at the bar, I tapped her on the shoulder, and was stunned to see a bruise over her eye.

'My God, have you fallen over?' I asked.

'No, I just hit her,' said her husband.

'Whatever for?'

''Cos she made a fool of you up there.'

I couldn't believe it.

'But it was all part of the act. It *was supposed* to be like that – honestly.'

'That's your trouble, Tom – you're all heart.'

Since any further attempt to explain could only lead to aggravation, I left it at that. The fact is, you never know what people may be thinking. I remember being followed along the promenade in Blackpool by a little old lady. Boy she was old. You wouldn't hit her age in three darts.

After about two hundred yards, she said: 'Excuse me, but it is you isn't it?'

'Yes,' I said, trying to look the part of the modest star.

'I thought it was. When are you coming back to finish the bathroom?' Exit modest star.

But we've all suffered the crushing put-down. Ask anyone who's worked Glasgow Empire on a Saturday night. I was lucky: I pretended to be Irish. At least it gave me a slight head start. Not like one poor soul. He'd gone through the basic opening of his act: song 'On a wonderful day like today'. Silence. Then three topical gags told with gusto and finesse. Silence. Then his tap-dance routine. Deafening silence! What to do next? He marched off stage, only to return carrying a trumpet.

'My God,' said an awestruck voice in the front row, 'Is there no end to this man's talent?'

When it's not your night it's not your night. Please, Lord, save me from fire, pestilence, hecklers and fights. Club fights are probably the biggest dread of an entertainer especially if they explode during his act. I've been lucky. The biggest one I've witnessed came out of nothing and had the most amazing ending.

It was in a district of Liverpool called Kirkby at a Catholic church club on a Saturday night: a packed house filling an L-shaped room – a virtual tennis match in terms of performing. One gag to the right, then one to the left. Stay cool – talk slow, easy does it. It worked for me – half an hour of fun and I was back behind a pint of Guinness waiting to see the singer. And then, just as the guy came on, the fight started. One side stood up and ran at the other side. Something to do with football, I think.

In about 0.01 of a second the room resembled a battlefield. Tables were overturned, chairs smashed, blood and bodies all over the place. Then it happened. At the height of the fray a little priest, about 5 foot tall, walked on stage, took off his collar and coat and dived into the fight. At the same time a man the size of Arnold Schwartzenegger, with a face full of scars, walked to the mike and said, 'Anybody who hits the Holy Father answers to me!'

Immediately the whole room froze. Apprehensive faces stared at the stage. Nobody moved – except the priest. He went round the room belting various men in the face, getting no reaction from them because of fear of the big guy at the mike. 'Sure, the Holy Father loves a good scrap,' said the little Irish housekeeper at my side.

'I'm not surprised. Nobody can hit him back,' I said, wondering at the strange state of affairs, and thinking that nothing else could surprise me. But I was wrong. As long as there are folk, there's no such thing as predictability. So let me give you some more examples that I was lucky to witness.

When an artist can guarantee Friday and Saturday bookings each week, he is a very contented 'turn'. When midweek dates start to flood in, he really has made it. The reason is that anything midweek has to be a private function – usually a corporate affair or a special presentation night. In my time I've been lucky to play at many of these, and in general they are much of a muchness. The essence of the job is a pre-show briefing: lists of the names of the main characters present and their idiosyncrasies are vital, and usually you are sent these details weeks before you appear. The worst type of job is the last-minute booking, usually to replace a comic who's dropped out. I have vivid memories of one such.

I was working in a church club in Birkenhead, hoping to amuse a room full of pigeon racers. Just before I was due to start my act, the phone rang. It was my agent, who said:

'If you can make the Grafton Ballroom by 11 o'clock, you're on fifty quid. What do you reckon?'

'For fifty quid I'd *crawl* to the Grafton. Tell them it's on.'

The brief was that there was a private function in the Grafton's Normandie Suite. Men only. Just get straight in and straight on. Cash on the night. The pigeon fanciers were only too delighted to help. They had me on, off and in the car before 10.15 pm, and I was through the Mersey Tunnel and back in the 'Pool well ahead of schedule.

The Grafton Rooms was a great entertainment complex, and I've many fond memories of weekend dances there. Ah, sweet days of my youth, when we all thought we could drink ten pints of beer, but generally collapsed in a heap after four or five. My pal's 21st birthday party ended with him walking out of the Grafton and straight into a pillar box. He felt it with both hands, followed it all the way round and said:

'My God – I've been walled in!'

Anyway, I found my way upstairs to the Normandie Suite where the room, far from being men only, was full of married couples – strange. However, the barman explained that my 'do' was in the annex – so in I went.

Surprise, surprise: it was certainly only men – only *three* men, to be exact. Two were from a company which made telephones, the third was from the GPO, who hopefully were going to put in a big equipment order. All the details and more were hurriedly given to me by one of the strippers, Elizabeth, a pal of mine, after her act:

'We've each done a spot, and we've done one together. We've tried everything but we can't get through to them. So good luck, Tom.'

With a gulp, not to mention a prayer, I went into a routine. One guy was from Scotland, so I tried a Scottish gag: he'd heard it. Then I tried a telephone gag – they'd *all* heard it. They seemed interested only in the table in front of them which was full of booze. Whisky, brandy, gin, pernod – even grenadine, for heaven's sake!

In desperation, I glanced around what was a very small room, and behold! – an upright piano. 'I'll tell you what, fellows,' I said, 'if I could play the piano I'd give you a song.'

'I can play,' said the man from the GPO. 'Why don't I give it a thrash?'

'You're on,' I said leading him to the piano and taking his place at the booze table.

An hour and a half later we'd sung every song we knew and some we didn't. Deals had been struck, phones had been ordered, and I'd had a skinful. I also had fifty pounds, plus a bonus of twenty for being a good comic.

Let me finish this chapter with a story Bob Monkhouse rates as one of my best but which also happens to be entirely true. The 007 Club in Burslem was much like other venues in the late '60s and early '70s: small, good atmosphere, with a gaming room and a late bar. Its major problem was that, in order to fulfil licensing laws, a cabaret had to perform even if no-one was listening – and, almost invariably, no-one *was* listening. The members would be grouped around the roulette wheel or card tables, and the acts were left to play to an empty room or the backs of bar staff heads. The exception to this was Thursdays. Thursdays were special. Thursdays were stag nights, and the concert room would be packed with noisy drunks who only wanted to see the strippers.

'We have three lovely ladies for you tonight, gentlemen,' the compère would intone in a phoney mid-atlantic accent. 'And remember, this isn't filth – it's art.' (If you believed that, you could nail jelly to the ceiling.)

The butt end of the stag night was that, in order to sell drinks, between the girls' strip teases, the rest of the acts had to perform five spots between them.

'Can you do three spots tonight?' asked the compère.

'Give me a break,' I said, 'I'm dying on my feet all week doing one!'

'All right. Tell you what. You do two and I'll get the speciality act to do three. Deal?'

'Deal!'

Speciality act? Speciality act? What sort of speciality act could do three shows to a crowd that looked like Vikings on the rampage? Magician? No! Juggler? No! Tumbler? – Surely not. Then what? Believe it or not, it was a strong man act. Now, I've seen a few of them. I had the pleasure once of working with a wonderful man called Henri Varden. He did a strength act dressed in a long bathing suit with a droopy false moustache, pretending he was a German. At the end of his very funny routine he would strap on a World War 1 German army helmet complete with spike. He would cue a drum roll and the crew would drop a full-sized cartwheel – over 200 pounds of wood and metal – out of the flies and on to his helmet. After the wheel had dropped, Henri, who seemed to have no neck, would spin it round, as the applause rang out and the curtains closed. What the audience didn't know was that, as the tabs shut, Henri's eyes would screw up in pain and he'd yell 'Jesus Christ!!' – every night. Funny, but nothing compared to Thursday at the 007 Club.

Failing volunteers from that night audience, or tracing the strippers whose named changed from Dominique to Doreen when they put their clothes back on, the only witness to my tale is Pat, my wife. She was there, she remembers. I didn't dream it. I went to the bar to join Pat watching The Great Beppo. His intro was a riot on its own. 'We've had this bloke here before,' said mid-atlantic accent. 'He didn't do well then, and to be honest I voted against him coming back. Still he's here. He's going to do three spots. Here's the first. The Great Beppo.' Silence, no applause, no play on – nothing. Just a very thin parting of the curtains and the light falling on the thinnest man I'd ever seen. Dressed in a leopardskin loin cloth, he looked like an anorexia victim. Not a pick on him.

'I've seen more meat on Lester Piggot's whip,' gasped a barmaid.

Beppo launched straight into his act – a display less of strength than of endurance – by pushing long needles into his cheeks. I winced, feeling the pain myself, as blood poured from each insertion. After eight or nine needles, and no crowd reaction, he took to chewing razor blades. You could hear them crunch at the back of the room. You could also see a trickle of blood from the corner of his mouth! To round off his first spot, our hero proceeded to break house bricks with his forehead. The bricks certainly did break, each leaving an ugly blue lump on his brow. Eventually he looked as if Santa's little helpers had battered his head with a million hammers!

Obviously in severe pain and in need of a blood

transfusion, Beppo exited to the sound of his own feet. And that was only the first show.

I followed quickly, and died the death of all time.

'Gerroff, and let's see the birds!'

'Give us a chance, lads.'

'Why? Nature didn't!' – Come back, Brennie McCormack.

Thank god the strippers went down well. They even promised something more exotic later, if the men would pass a glass round. I resolved to make sure I got on before that particular event.

Then on came Beppo for his second go. Wounds still leaking blood and bumps still swelling, he broke four pint glasses into very sharp bits and placed them on the floor. Next, he managed to find four huge men still sober enough to stand up, and led them on stage.

To mild interest, at least from the staff, Beppo got the four giants to stand on his chest as he lay prone on the glass. Drum roll, chord on organ – and dead silence. The four men left the stage and Beppo stood up, to reveal that his back was in ribbons – lacerated beyond recognition.

'Phoney!' called the front row as he bowed and then stumbled off.

'Whatever happens,' I said to Pat, 'we've got to wait and see what he follows this with.'

In my second spot I didn't do so badly. I made a couple of remarks about the razor blades and glass and they seemed to be received well enough. After a couple of songs, including 'You'll never walk alone', I was off with my wits intact and the full fee in my pocket.

Now for the big moment. I think the management were as curious as me because they delayed the erotic show in order to let Beppo do his third turn. And what a turn! On he came dressed immaculately in frilly front shirt, dickie bow, dress suit and patent leather shoes. His face and mouth still showed blood, albeit congealing, and his forehead looked like a model of the Himalayas.

He walked to the microphone, smiled and burst passionately into song: 'It's the good life . . .'

Even the hard nuts in the 007 finally cracked, and I reckon the strippers would have had a hard time following that. As for me and Pat, we laughed all the way home.

6

Generally, when I'm interviewed in the press or on TV I'm referred to as an amalgam of TV host, game show compère, comedian and author. Although all these hats fit, I still regard myself as a very lucky ex-teacher. Lucky because I am doing what I love most and being paid to do it.

But luck doesn't have to come with money. In the long run luck is all about health, happiness, a great family, and the chance to meet some amazing characters – and I've met more than my share, I can tell you. Throughout my career of thirty-odd years there have been people in my life that even Hollywood couldn't invent.

Let me introduce some of my favourite folk to you. In my earliest days in showbusiness, I may have been a hard-bitten teacher, but I was a highly impressionable singer, I suppose my first great character was Les Radcliffe. Les was manager of the Selwyn, a pub near Liverpool's Anfield stadium and scene of my first professional engagement as a country-and-western singer. These were the days of the double act of 'Tom and Brennie', and Les engaged us at £2 per night for two nights a week. We shared our pay with Eddie Farrell, our 'manager' and 'roadie', and we spent many happy hours singing and trying out patter in this most jolly of pubs. The clientèle on Saturdays and Sundays were locals interspersed with match-goers, and win or lose it was money for booze. We used to offer a pint to any member of the audience who could name a song we couldn't either sing or accompany, and in three years the only one that stumped us was 'A little box of pine on the 7.29', possibly the worst song ever written.

Les Radcliffe was great. He and his wife Hilda really looked after Brennie and me as if we were their sons. Hilda's speciality meal, spare ribs and butter beans, used to be the talk of the town and were a delight when washed down with a few pints of bitter. She and Les had met many years before in Liverpool on New Year's Eve while waiting for the midnight chimes, and Hilda asked Les for a light for her cigarette. Every New Year's Eve since then, no matter whether together or a thousand miles apart, they would each light a cigarette on the stroke of midnight – even after they'd given up smoking! There's a loving memory.

I have loving memories of them both, starting with Les's first instruction to us:

'Get here about a late half eight, lads.'

'What about twenty to nine?'

'No, before that!'

Les was only too eager to let us go when better work came along, but he was always there when work and money were short and we needed a job. Bless you both and may the Lord smile on you always.

Les was our first boss, and there were to be many more. Professionally speaking, each one was as important as the next because no matter what the level of entertainment or the size of your fee, every job was vital to my way up the showbiz ladder. The 'wannabees', and 'gonnabees' are 'nobodies' if they only believe their own publicity. Each person in the business is as important as the other and there is nothing more important than finding the right agent or manager. In my time I've had a few, and known many more but some, indeed most, fade into the past whilst others will stay evergreen.

Mary Wills, a very special lady, was the first agent to find me work when I went solo. Let me admit at once that in those early days my act was dreadful – and that was on a good day! Having built my repertoire in the Selwyn before a home-grown crowd, I thought I was ready for the heavy duty working men's and social clubs, but I was wrong. Too gentle by half, my mixture of folk and country-and-western songs and wry witticisms were not 'front foot enough' and needed improving in the hotbed of Saturday nights before 'we've seen it all' audiences. Mary gave me the chance to do this and persevered, when others said the worst about the act.

'Keep going, lad,' she urged, 'and you'll get it right – even if it kills us both.'

I kept going. It didn't kill either of us but I sometimes worried about Mary. She'd a weird way of describing her ailments – probably some Irish in her.

'How are you, Mary?'

'Well it's all over now. Me arms, me shoulders, me chest – absolute agony. Walking miracle, the doctor says.'

'But in yourself?'

'Oh, in meself I'm fine!!'

How I mused over that line. I mean how can you ache all over and be fine in yourself? God knew, Mary knew, her husband Jimmy knew. And all three are together now.

Another man who knew of Mary's ailments was Ernie Mack, one of the top entrepreneurs of his day. Ernie has retired from the hurly burly of showbiz, although he still puts on the odd show featuring old favourites, not to mention his banjo.

The Broadway Club and the Montrose Club in Whitefield Road, have seen thousands of spectaculars produced, directed and hosted by Ernie Mack, who knew what the public wanted and never failed to give it to them. Appearances on his shows gained me a spell on *The Comedians* series, and eventually led to my being chosen to appear on *Opportunity Knocks*, the show which was my launching pad to the big time. Advice and expertise were always within reach when Ernie was around, and he and Billy 'Uke' Scott were the prime movers in the early development of my 'home-spun look-at-life' type of act. 'Why bother trying to conquer the world? Why not become a big fish in the Liverpool pool and then wait for the world to come to you?' Sound advice from Billy, a star in his own right and epitome of all things professional.

'A pro never turns his back on an audience.'

'A pro goes on, to die if necessary, but never bemoans his fate.'

Ernie, too, had some great lines mostly to do with cash-flow problems:

'Look, Tommy, I can't pay a fortune, but when you're not working even a bottle of Guinness is profit, isn't it?' (Er, not quite.) Or:

'I've got you a little job on the island of Gan. It's not a lot of money, but you'll be seen.' (Gan, a tiny dot in the middle of the Indian Ocean, was an RAF base: not exactly a staging post en route to the London Palladium.)

The biggest laugh anyone got on one of Ernie's shows was to say: 'And I'd like to thank Ernie Mack for proving to me that money isn't everything.'

Still you've got to remember that dealing with artistes is only half of the work of the promoter. The difficult side of the job is handling bookers and club owners – men like Harry Millhouse. I'm glad to say that, for some unknown reason, Harry Millhouse was a fan of mine. (If he didn't like you, then gawd help you, you got no work on his patch.)

Harry was the original owner of the Montrose Club. In its early days it was a members only set up and it had started – like a good many of its clientèle – when Adam was a lad. The concert room and bar were situated at the top of a very high, narrow staircase and it was as hard to reach as was the funny bone of the audience. Here were people whose priorities were wonderfully straightforward. Not for them such issues as the state of the economy, nuclear testing, British foreign policy and men on the moon. The typical conversation with the club owner usually began like this. 'Harry, we've had a word with all the regulars and we want to know why you've raised the price of a pint to 1s/10d.' 'Because I didn't have the heart to raise it to two bob!' came the caustic put down.

Harry had an apparently limitless fund of one liners that stopped you dead in your tracks. Have you ever ridden a bicycle and had the misfortune to lose the front wheel while going at speed? No? Well what happens is that for about $1\frac{1}{2}$ seconds the bike stays upright and on course and then ever so slowly you sink to the ground, usually in the grinding flurry of flesh, bones and spokes. Harry could do that to you with a tongue lashing. Witness this call to Ernie Mack.

'That comic we had last night, Ernie: I want him back for New Year's Eve and I'll pay whatever you say.'

'Oh, that's nice Harry. What time would you like him there?'

'Oh, I'll want him all night. He won't be going on stage. I just want to make sure he's out of the way so he doesn't ruin anyone's bloody New Year!!'

When the Montrose Club electronic organ went on the blink, a repair man was sent round and he put it right in a couple of minutes. He charged £5 as a call out fee, and Harry assumed that was that. But oh no! comes the end of the month he was sent a labour and parts bill for 67 quid. So a little call to the organ company was in order:

'Hello, is that Rushworth and Dreaper?'

'Yes, sir.'

'Is it true you installed that great organ in the new Catholic cathedral?'

'That's correct, sir.'

'Well, you've sent the bloody bill to me, mate!'

He'd got a way with words, had Harry. I missed him when he retired to the Isle of Man.

It was on that fair island that I bumped into Tommy Leddy, the finest road manager I ever had, and the funniest. Years before, Tommy had been our family butcher when we lived in Formby. He'd retired and spent his days in the Conservative Club playing snooker, a game he was 'ace' at (whence my nickname for him). Ace's wife Theresa had four children and the eldest girl, Janet, happened to be one of my dancers in a summer show we'd cobbled together for the Gaiety Theatre, Douglas, in 1975. It was a very successful season and left me with great memories and lots of laughs. I recall the Irish arriving in their thousands and bringing with them, I'm sure quite unwittingly, many hundreds of forged five-pound notes. Before we had time to cross check numbers with the police we'd already taken about £200 at the box office. This called for drastic action and outriders were sent to various parts of the known world to buy boxes of matches and return with pockets full of loose change but kosher money.

Tommy and Theresa helped out with all the dreary day-consuming chores that lie behind a successful theatre show and were more like family than friends. So it followed as night follows day that, when we returned to the mainland and a heavy pressure of work built up, Tommy became my driver, confidante, personal assistant and buddy. Ace and I went there and back, we hit a few walls on the way but we survived and we had fun. We went there, we saw that, we heard every gag, we fought every foe, we smiled many a smile, we shed many tears – but they were usually tears of laughter.

One night we were in the theatre tavern opposite the ABC Theatre in Yarmouth when I was approached by a typical bar fly on the cadge for the price of a pint. He gave me all the schmaltzy chat: 'I'm your biggest fan ... always watch your shows ... there'll never be another like you' – you know the sort of thing.

'Oi!' said Ace Leddy. 'What are you after, chum?'

'The loan of a fiver, mate.'

'Well, let me explain something to you. There's lots of needy people in this hard old world, and I'm one. So if the boss has any spare fivers they're bloody well coming to me!'

Yes, Tommy too had ways of expressing himself – sometimes without resorting to words. Take the night we had 'the mooners'. Let me explain that in pantomimes I did a sketch which involved the firing of a very loud revolver. For safety's sake I never left it in the theatre, taking it home with me after every show. One night, after leaving the Empire Theatre, Liverpool, we stopped at traffic lights and were approached by four drunks, who suddenly turned their backs, dropped their drawers, and flashed their bottoms at us.

'Bang!' went the gun (firing a double charge of blanks) in Ace's hand.

'Cher-rist,' screamed the mooners as they tried to flee with clothes around ankles.

'That'll learn yer,' bellowed Tommy. 'You dirty articles.'

Mind you, Tommy was not totally immune from embarrassment himself. I'm thinking of the time I was in London recording a series of 'London Night Out', a spectacular variety show with a game in the middle called 'Name that Tune'. Accommodation – a suite of rooms no less – was provided at the Drury Lane Hotel every Sunday. It was more than welcome after a five-hour drive down from my summer season in Blackpool, and it enabled us to relax and recharge the batteries.

Tommy and I had already had a funny do the week before when, in order to show us how the closed circuit TV worked, a night porter took us down to the car park in the lift. On the way back the lift jammed between floors and, after we had pressed the alarm button and used the emergency phone, we were winched back to normality by the oddest rescue team you've ever seen: an Egyptian, a Jamaican, a one-armed Irishman and a peculiar character wearing eye makeup and possessing the world's worst stammer. Once we were out of the lift, they pressed me for a group photo to be taken. God knows what people thought if they ever saw a copy of it.

Anyway, Pat accompanied us the next weekend, so it meant that there was no bed for Ace. He, being typically Scouse, would not hear of my paying for an extra room. Instead, he insisted that he spent the night on the couch in the lounge. I suppose after a sufficient intake of Scotch, all places are home, and it was too late to argue. Be that as it may, at 5.30 am my roadie woke with an urgent need to go to the loo. One minute he lay in the arms of Morpheus, clad only in his leopardskin underpants (bikini cut) which Theresa had bought him. Seven and a half stones of British Beef, not quite Mr Puniverse, but not Arnie Schwartzenegger either; the next he was seized by an imperious call of nature. Rolling out of bed, he groped his way towards the bathroom door. Softly, so's not to waken Pat and me, he turned the knob, slid inside and gently closed the door behind him. Too late! He suddenly was aware of a light he'd not switched on. As he forced his eyelids fully open, he realised (a) that he was not in the bathroom but in the hotel corridor, and (b) that he was face to face with the night porter on his fire round.

'Can I help you, sir?' (Great question, that.)

'I'm trying to get in here,' spluttered Ace.

'But that's Mr and Mrs O'Connor's room.'

'I know, but I'm in there with them.'

'Oh, really, and can you identify yourself, sir?'

With very little in the way of wallet, passport, or credit cards, Tommy pulled open the waistband of the leopardskin underpants, glanced down and said, 'Yes, that's me.' Who could argue?

Funny man, Tommy: a good friend, but a mischievous little devil. At his best when you're at your worst. Beware him when you've had one too many: he can drink you under the table and then take advantage of you. Who but he would think of the snooker table routine? We'd watched and waited while two old codgers drank themselves into near oblivion at the Formby Conservative Club. As they reloaded their glasses at the bar, Tommy slipped an extra red ball into one of the pockets of the snooker table. Now, have you ever seen two drunks trying to put 16 reds in a triangle? It went on forever and included such cogent instructions as: 'Don't start at the pointed end.' Obviously, by this time the ancient pair had taken so much on board that they could see only one corner of the triangle at a time.

But it's a wondrous sight to behold and gets so serious that no one wants to admit responsibility for fear of being blamed for a resultant heart attack! Tommy, 'Ace', you're a gem. You're a one-off, you're not a credit to the profession – you're an example to be copied and held dear. May you enjoy many years, decades or whatever, in hard-earned retirement.

I know that in venues all over the world right this minute there are colourful people whose deeds and misdeeds will be extolled by people like me for years to come. None the more, like many before me, I've got to believe that they don't make them like they did in my day.

There was little George at Allinson's theatre club. Ostensibly, he was back-stage manager, a grand title but basically the man who tidied everywhere up, made sure there was soap in the dressing room and paper in the loo. George was four feet ten inches of fun, a retired comic of seventy plus years who was game for any on or off stage prank. I used him for years as a planted heckler who would eventually storm on to the stage, only to be thrown all over the place with an Irish whip wrestling throw. It looked like pensioner-bashing, but he could fall into a judo roll and feel no pain.

Great theatre, particularly when he stormed off mouthing abuse and I would say: 'he's in such a temper, he's going to stamp up and down *under* the tables all night!'

Good old George, whose only perk was on Sunday lunch when he got to collect the strippers' discarded clothes and take them back to their naked owners' dressing rooms.

If Allinson's had George, the Wooky Hollow had Jimmy 'Spot'. As his nickname suggests, Jimmy was in charge of the lights at this premier Liverpool night spot. The Wooky Hollow was a legendary club which in its time featured the very highest in the showbusiness hierarchy – Jack Jones, Shirley Bassey and countless other luminaries. All who played the club agreed that it was second to none. None more than me on my first engagement there.

To ensure a clear run on the Sunday night, the management insisted on a 'band-call' or rehearsal at about 4 pm on the Sunday afternoon. This was a rotten time as you can imagine. Out-of-town acts arriving from all over the place had to book into digs, unpack, grab a snack and drag themselves into a dark, smoke-filled, beer-drenched room and try to give of their best. What baffles me, even as a local, was that we'd rehearse on Sunday afternoon with a pianist we didn't see again till Friday night. Apparently, he would ring the other keyboard men after the rehearsal and tell them what to play. What a carry on! But that was only the start of my problems.

On my first night I was lucky to be introduced by a great compère, Bobby Shack, who was kindness itself to me. I learned a lot from this man who loved comedy and loved people.

'Remember, son,' he would say, 'one-third of your audience can't hear you very well, one third can't see you very well, and the others don't need preaching at: they just want to relax and enjoy your company.'

How right he was. Audiences can sense fear, they can tell
when an artiste is unsure. So my first objective was to make
them relax and give them the confidence to laugh, or not to
laugh, whenever they wanted. And they would have laughed
plenty had they known of my plight that first Sunday. With
30 seconds to go to my debut, I was feeling cool and looking
good. Brand new charcoal-grey suit, new dress shirt and
bow tie, squeaky clean shoes. With 25 seconds to go, I was
a mess. A well-meaning drunk had staggered up to wish me
all the best by shaking my hand and punching me playfully
in the chest. What he'd forgotten was the pint of mild in
his left fist. As he punched me, the beer splashed right down
the front of my trousers. I was soaked.

'Quick,' said my pal Tony West. 'Put mine on.'

So there in the semi-darkness of a crowded club, before
many hundreds of eyes, I changed pants with Tony while
our drunken friend made a 'wall' with his coat to cover our
embarrassment. 'And here he is, our special guest,' said
Bobby Shack (as I struggled with the belt buckle). 'Give him
a real Wooky welcome,' (as I wrestled with the zip). 'Tom
O'Connor!' I was moving at speed, but trying to look cool.
God knows how the trousers looked. They were bright
green and must have clashed with the charcoal grey coat.
But if I thought I looked daft, I was relieved to look through
the glare at Jimmy 'Spot'. He'd made the ultimate sacrifice:
to enable Tony West to return to his seat with dignity,
Jimmy had lent him *his* trousers!

So there stood our hero, behind the spotlight six feet up
on a ladder, dressed in dinner jacket, bow tie, polka-dot
boxer shorts, and socks with suspenders. Ah, Jimmy boy –
what you did for me, old pal!

It's true that money can't buy love. Love is something
special: it is the food of memories. Memories have to be
earned, have to be so vivid that all time is present, all people
are young and nobody dies. Memories can be enjoyed at

any time and they allow us to be selective: we can chose what and what not to recall – we can alter history. My dad does that. He recounts World War 2 from a totally different angle to the historians. If Montgomery and Eisenhower had only known the talents of my dad and his pals they'd have slept easier in their beds. Although an infantryman turned anti-aircraft gunner, dad also trained with the Special Boat Squadron.

'But you can't swim,' I objected.

'You didn't have to in the war.' (Um – can we have that again, more slowly?)

He tells a good tale, though, about landing on the French beaches following a barrage by the 15-inch guns of HMS *Rodney*, which hit targets 20 miles inland. As they made their way into the French hinterland, an irate farmer bellowed and gesticulated at them, and pointed to his burning barn.

'Not us, mate,' said one squaddie. 'It's that bloody great ship out there!'

Whilst every member of my family is good for a memorable tale, the one who is a legend in clubland is my wife Pat. When I first worked outside Liverpool as a TV name, it was to headline a show at Jollees Club at Longton, near Stoke-on-Trent. I was delighted to find that the guest star was Ronnie Hilton – a fine singer, and what an act. The club was beautiful – the best venue, front and back-stage, at which I have ever appeared. The dressing rooms were like suites in a Park Lane hotel. The staff were hand-picked and made sure we wanted for nothing. The management had thought of everything, right down to drinks order forms on each table so that people could watch the show undisturbed by the nattering of punters and waitresses. There were suggestion forms for the artistes to fill in if we could think of improvements. I never could. They'd thought of everything. And they thought they'd seen everything until the moment came to pay me.

'Give it to Pat,' I said. 'She's the governor.'

'How would you like it, love? It's a thousand pounds plus VAT. Do you want a cheque or cash.'

'Well, I don't care about the rest of it,' said Pat, 'but I'll want five pounds in 10p pieces for the kids' dinner money.'

Thus spake a true Yorkshire woman, mother and ex-teacher. Henceforward I was known as the act who worked for dinner money.

7

So much, for the moment, for the backstage characters in my life. What about the names and faces that shared the footlights with me? What of sung and unsung heroes and heroines who, every day and every night, try to brighten the lives of the hardworking populace. Where shall I start? Well, what about the greatest of the smallest – Arthur Askey. Arthur was the purveyor of wondrous tales, true and almost true, told with perfect timing. Before I attempt to relate his Bournemouth tale, let me remind you of the man: barely five feet tall, huge horn-rimmed glasses with bottle-bottom lenses and a very distinctive gait. In a word, unmistakable – or so one would think.

Arthur had been engaged by a corporate group to perform at the Bath Hotel in Bournemouth. A good fee, overnight accommodation and breakfast were part of the deal, and the little man arrived in mid-afternoon to check in. On his way up, he was joined in the lift by another guest.

'Hello, Arthur,' he said.

'Hello,' said Askey.

'I bet everyone calls you that – you don't half look like him, you know.'

'Do I? Well I never,' said Arthur, straight-faced.

That night he wowed them in the hotel's crowded conference room. Next morning, descending in the lift, he was joined by the guest from the day before.

'Morning, Arthur,' he said. 'You won't believe it, but he was here last night, you know.'

A good tale, 'Wave'. ('Wave' was what Arthur's daughter called him because, for many years, all she ever saw of him was an arm waving out of a railway carriage window as he thundered by on his way to another show. 'There's your daddy – wave!' said her mother. So 'Wave' he became.) Nice to have met you my little friend, you were a genius and a gentleman and we're all the poorer since you left us.

With a promise that I will tell tales of other entertainers in due course, let me stay with comedy for a while and talk about a man who for years has excelled in all forms of the art. From children's shows, to family shows, to all-male after-dinner shows, Leslie Crowther has no betters. A raucous laugh, a retentive memory and a wonderful delivery make him the perfect man for the job. To see him work you'd think he'd never had a bad night in his career. No-one would be that good and struggle on stage, surely? Not so, according to the man himself. While we all have a 'died-the-death' epic in our repertoire, Les seems to have reserved his worst times for the very best occasions. Well, you can't find a posher floor to fall flat on than the Savoy Grill in London.

The Savoy is a very prestigious booking – not earned easily or accepted lightly. When I was honoured with three weeks' work there I soon learned the rules that apply when entertaining the gentry. Bearing in mind that the audiences do not know who will be on when they book a meal, it is important that nobody overstays their welcome. So Frank Sinatra, Madonna or Tom O'Connor – the time given for a cabaret is twenty-five minutes only.

'Sometimes that'll feel like a week,' said the band-leader. How right he was. Most nights were unbelievably easy, just occasionally you got a room full of foreigners or, worse still, the uninterested. The late Dickie Henderson told a story of the roller-skating act who was constantly heckled by an ancient dowager who had, as they say, taken drink. In desperation, the skater grabbed her and dragged her on stage to do the audience participation. This included being gripped under the arms and spun round at lightning speed. After ten seconds of rotation the lady's bladder yielded to pressure, and she relieved herself at great speed over the front tables.

Leslie Crowther didn't quite get that reaction, but a similar lady was involved. Because of fears of confrontations between acts and audience, a strict house rule stated that artistes must not enter the cabaret area or the front of the hotel while engaged at the hotel, but must come and go through a rear door. Sensible rule it seemed to me, and applicable to everyone at all times except for one L Crowther esquire.

It was the time of the first heart transplants, when the pioneer Dr Christian Barnard had his picture everywhere, and was everywhere feted. One member of Dr Barnard's staff was apparently a dead ringer of Leslie, and one evening the doctor, his team and several guests were seated in the Savoy and had requested that Leslie Crowther join them for a photo.

The management decided, just this once, to allow the artiste to come through the main room after his show and join Barnard in the foyer of the hotel. Now, wouldn't you know: Leslie picked that night of all nights to bomb totally on stage. No laughs, no smiles, no reaction but apathy and bored hostility. Off he swept, hoping *not* to be called back for another bow, and waiting for the ground to swallow him up.

'Don't forget your photo date,' he was painfully reminded.

So, breathing deeply, he plunged through the pass door into the main room, head down, and tried to look like someone else as he made for the other end.

'Hey, you,' screamed an old dear dressed in *all* the family jewellery, including tiara. 'Yes, you,' she insisted. 'You were rubbish.'

Just what Leslie needed. 'You were absolute crap. Wasn't he?' she shouted to the surrounding tables. 'Wasn't he the worst thing you've ever seen?'

'Yes,' came the ever-growing chorus.

Les tried to ignore her and carry on walking. But she persisted, grabbing his sleeve and hanging on as he accelerated to maximum walking speed.

'You were nothing but tripe from start to finish. Wouldn't pay you in washers. You're the pits ...'

She was dragged the full length of the Savoy Grill at prodigious speed by the most red-faced man in history. As he rounded the corner to safety and the welcoming arms of Dr Barnard, the lady was freed from his arms and led away still screaming. 'And another thing ...'

Yes, the punter *can* be an oddity, but then so can the celebrity. Ask Marti Caine. Among the great female entertainers my lovely Marti ranks very high. Comedienne, singer, chat show and game show hostess, the lady has done it all and done it superbly. Never stuck for a one liner, a quick riposte, or an instant put down if necessary, she was once caught totally gob smacked by a living legend. It was at the press launch for the return of *The King and I* to the West End stage, featuring the great Yul Brynner. As press functions go, it was quite a splendid affair: champagne, caviar, various delights in the finger buffet, celebrities a-plenty and a good healthy buzz. But there *were* problems of logistics. For instance, if you're not a drinker (and Marti isn't) but you are a smoker (and Marti is), you can end up with a glass of champagne in one hand, an unlit cigarette in the other and no means of striking a match to light it. So there she stood, radiant, immaculately dressed and sporting $1\frac{1}{2}$ inch long false finger nails seeming a little like a damsel in distress. Then suddenly it happened. In swept Brynner, coat over shoulders, every inch a star, and very aware of all around him, even to the extent of noticing the plight of the stunning redhead. So as he passed by, he whipped out a butane gas lighter and flicked it in Marti's direction. She attempted to make contact between cigarette and inch-high flame. Unfortunately, the flame missed the fag but found her finger nails, which immediately caught fire, leaving her no option but to douse them in her glass of champagne. Meantime the Great Yul had gone by, not knowing he'd left Marti with nails gnarled and welded together!

How I love those stories. And how I love to tell them. But, more importantly, how I love to be able to say 'I was there'.

I remember Demis Roussos and I'm pretty sure he'll remember me if he is reminded of this incident. We were recording my TV series at the New London Theatre in Drury Lane, but it was during troubled times. We were in the middle of several industrial disputes, one involving the power unions at a national level, and a local one affecting the TV electrics. On the day Demis was to appear as top of the bill he was brought to the studio in a plush limo, and he and his manager joined me in the green room. Demis was dressed in calf-high boots and a huge fur coat that reached virtually to his ankles. His dresser carried a bag full of caftans for the act.

'He won't need those,' I explained 'We won't be recording this evening.' The power cut in our area had made it impossible to use our cameras. We had, however, arranged to put on a sort of show just for the poor old studio audience who had travelled many miles to be there. Using safety lights and very underpowered microphones we struggled to entertain. Demis did his act in his fur coat, but nobody had explained to him why. He thought he'd done the real thing.

Four weeks later we re-booked the show. But this time our own 'sparks' were in dispute and again we had a 'make-do-and-mend' affair of it. Again Demis wore his fur coat – presumably thinking we were doing a re-take.

Two weeks later, and all the union troubles resolved, we assembled to do the show for real. Could we get Roussos to take off his fur coat? No way.

'It was good enough for the last two shows. It's good enough for this one,' he insisted. Exit a confused Greek, a fine entertainer, but a man who would certainly give me the swerve if he saw me again.

Apart from pantomimes, or having them as guests on TV shows, my dealings with actors are few and far between. Shame really because I so admire their expertise, their gift of being able to perform exactly the same lines time after time and make it appear to be the first time. I sit enthralled when they relate stories of their profession. How wonderful to be able to quote the greatest names in theatrical history and link a happening to them.

Sir Ralph Richardson was apparently touring with a not-so-good play and was obviously irked by it. So during one matinée he suddenly blurted an unscripted line, 'Is there a doctor in the house?'

'I'm a doctor, sir,' came a voice from the stalls.

'Isn't this an awful play, doctor?' said Sir Ralph. Magic!

Then there was the other knight of the boards who, for mischief, I shall leave nameless. He was touring a small repertory company performing Shakespeare. Three days, one play, three days another, travel to another town on Sunday. On Wednesday night he began his curtain speech.

'We hope you've enjoyed our performance of *Hamlet*, and if you're interested, the same company will be here tomorrow evening performing *Macbeth*. My wife will be playing the part of Lady Macbeth ...'

He was interrupted by a voice from the gods, 'Your wife is a big, fat, ugly cow.'

'Nevertheless,' said the knight, 'she will be here ...'

I like the cool way he chose not to argue with the description.

Lest I become too involved with the big names, let me

mention a couple of the unsung heroes of our business. One of my particular favourites is a close friend called Gil Dova, an American juggler who currently appears in Las Vegas, but who for many years was a brilliant member of my summer season team. Gil's from a showbusiness family, his father (a survivor of the 1937 *Hindenburg* airship disaster) being what used to be called an 'eccentric comedian'. Gil is married to Regina Baranton, one of two beautiful French twins who performed a foot juggling act, spinning barrels, planks and even tables and then flicking them from one to another. While Regina practised with her feet, Gil manipulated balls, clubs, blocks and virtually anything else he could find while standing on a narrow plinth several feet in the air. I loved the way he had a suitable gag to cover any dropped prop or other disaster. He even had a small notebook on juggling which he would take out of his pocket and study earnestly before going on. My lasting memory of the man was the birth of his first child, Henry. We were in a huge summer show at the Opera House at Blackpool in 1979, and Regina was much (in fact, *very* much) with child. As Gil prepared to go on she warned:

'I can feel the baby coming.'

'Can you wait six minutes?' was all Gil had time to say before his music played him on.

Well, she couldn't. And at the end of the show, in our final 'walkdown', the band leader held up a large card bearing the announcement: 'It's a boy!'

8

___

Years of bitter experience have taught me the truth of two sporting adages: 'You make your own luck' and 'The more you practice, the luckier you get'.

But I also believe that the Almighty gives us not what we want, but what we need. And in the serious business of comedy the major need is close support. In my thirty-odd years in showbusiness I've sometimes been let down badly by people I trusted, but I've always been able to rely on firm family support. Funny people, or rather people who try to be funny for a living, need a solid base from which to chance their arm. My old saying in times of strife was 'If I don't go well in this place, I don't want to come back anyway – and besides, think of all the nice places I *can* go back to.' This worked after a fashion, but my greatest comfort, especially in the early days was: 'I don't have to rely on this job – I'm also a brilliant teacher.' Unfortunately, that wasn't true. I was a competent teacher in my day, but I wouldn't last a week in the modern set up.

Then I'd met my lovely Pat at a training college dance and knew at once I would marry her: it was love at first sight. To prove my love was strong I actually proposed while watching a film called *The man who could cheat death* – surely that's a cue for a gag. We wed in 1962 in Keighley and I spent the first three hours of married life playing football in the street with about 40 of the wedding guests, not all of them men, and not all of them sober.

Our honeymoon was a disaster because the people in the guest house at Grange over Sands knew we were newly weds and made it obvious. It meant we had to sit up all night listening to them rabbit on about motorbikes, blood sports and the price of pigs even though we genuinely only wanted to sleep. At night there was still no rest as our bedroom, away from the rest of the guests out of deference to our new status, was situated next to the toilet which had a flushing system all its own: two slow pulls, a quick one and another slow one was the combination. It was hysterical with one couple because the wife used to squeak down the steps, use the loo, and squeak back upstairs, whereupon her husband had to come downstairs to flush it. We told the landlady of the problem and she said, 'It's always been like that. My best advice is to sneak up and surprise it!'

Leaving the guest-house two days earlier than scheduled, we went back to Bootle to a house my parents had bought us. It was ready furnished, which was a blessing, but there were one or two problems. The previous owner had been a DIY buff and had personally repaired the roof. Unfortunately he'd not replaced the slates, but stuck them together with Polyfilla. It looked fine until it rained. And, boy, did it rain. It rained so hard it brought all the ceilings down. I was teaching in a junior mixed school with the pregnant Pat and we found a friend in Reg Baden, a great house renovator. Reg showed me how to remove old iron fire places, brick up the spaces and plaster over – make good as they say. I removed eight fire places and got 30 bob for each one at the scrap dealer (I'm sure he thought I was stealing the stuff). The money paid for timber and polystyrene tiles which I used to replace the ceilings and insulate the house. A few odd slates were put in place and home was sweet again.

Here we lived happily, raising Anne Marie and Stephen Joseph, and both of us still teaching at the same school. Pat

had the younger school children and I had the not-so-bright
ten year olds. 'My son's ten now and he can't even write
"cat". I can do better meself,' claimed one parent, who had
to excuse me as I gagged the laughter with my hanky. Then
there was the headmaster: 'Every boy and girl in this school
can be the best at something. Even you, Bernard Green!'
(Bernard enjoyed the unusual distinction of being thicker
than *three* short planks.)

'Yes, Bernard,' persisted the head, 'you could be the best
in the school at – er – er – um – er – walking to the toilet.'
My God, what had he said? For the rest of the term, I
couldn't keep the child in the classroom. He spent his entire
time marching to and fro; 'dry runs to the loos' the other
kids called it.

Bernard had a unique string to his bow: he was the most
qualified child never to pass the 11-plus exam. In my school-
days the exam system required that you read the English or
intelligence paper, read the questions, and then wrote the
answer. By the latter years of my teaching days the whole
thing had changed. Now, a selection of answers to a question
was given and the entrant had to underline the correct one.
So it was on a June day in 1964 that 'Benal Gern' (this is
how Bernard spelt his name) got the combination right. It
was a bit like winning the football pools. He underlined any
old answer, was finished in five minutes and had an IQ
(according to his guesses) in the region of 185. The headmaster was over the moon until I pointed out that 'mas-
termind' had not only spelt his name wrong but had written
it on the *back* of the paper not the front. Only by challenging
Bernard to read the questions out was the truth revealed.

Wasn't it John Dewey who said that written intelligence
tests for children who can't read are a bit like the way pigs
used to be weighed. The idea was to place a plank see-saw
fashion over a barrel, with the pig at one end. Next you
found a rock that balanced out the pig. Then you guessed
the weight of the rock!

A year after having Stephen, Pat delivered Frances, a baby who struggled with a peculiar blood group and bravely rode out two complete blood changes – ('blue babies' they were called in those days). Pat's group was B negative, mine was O positive and that was what caused the problem. Frances, or at least her imminent arrival, was the reason I entered the world of entertainment. With Pat giving up teaching and my wages only £7 per week, times were hard. I'll always remember the feeling of desperation when I went to the bank hoping to draw out £3 housekeeping money.

'Unfortunately,' said the cashier, 'we've paid your year's rates in one instalment instead of quarterly. Sorry about that. You still have a one shilling balance, but you must leave it there to keep your account open.'

Sorry they may have been, but not as sorry as me. We had crisp sandwiches for two days and made food for the babies from the best of what was left in the fridge. Eddie Farrell, my butcher pal, let me help out in his shop. I worked all day on Saturday (12 hours) for a joint of lamb for Sunday. But the next thing we knew, Eddie had talked Les Radcliffe into letting me and Brennie McCormack do a spot at the Selwyn pub. The die was cast!

People sometimes ask me, 'What does it take to give you the hard skin of a comic? What can give you the motivation to stand your ground and die the death because the audience are drunk, or ignorant, or totally uninterested?' My answer is, 'It takes the memory of two hungry babies and a hungry wife heavy with a third. It's amazing the guts you can draw from that.'

Strangely, my family became my greatest fans. You would think they would hate any job that took dad away from home at night. But quite the reverse was true. They loved the tales I told of late night adventures, the songs I learned and practised on them, the Christmas parties I took them to at factories and clubs. Some years they saw at least one Santa per day. All of these were much the same; except maybe for Joe. Joe was an 80-year-old member of a British Legion club in Lancashire whom the management had recklessly offered £5 and all he could drink to dress up as Father Christmas. Joe immediately made huge inroads into the club's Guinness stocks and within an hour was on stage, legless, witless, and sporting natural grey hair and a false beard stained by the black stuff. Not content to distribute the presents, Santa attempted to lead the bemused youngsters in several carols and Christmas hits, while stumbling around knocking over mike stands, aspidistras and footlights.

'Ee, look at Santa – he's drunk, dad,' said young Stephen O'Connor, wise beyond his years.

'No, no, – he's just not feeling well,' said his protective dad. 'He's got the flu.'

'Ay, and if he has one more glass of flu I'll bloody brain him,' said the club steward.

Funny that my only son should be involved with a drunk at the tender age of three. Maybe he recognised a little of himself in the inebriated old man. It came about like this. Because of money shortages and very heavy outgoings for baby wear, baby food and babies generally, it became physically and economically impossible for Pat and me to have a good night out together. So all free evenings were spent at home watching TV or entertaining friends. They were great times when I think back. Trading tales, singing songs (folk and protest types) and planning how to reshape the world. Seven pint cans of beer at today's equivalent of 65p were a must at these 'dos'. Sometimes we went so far as to take the empty cans, or even a spare tin bath, to the pub to have a refill from the draught bitter tap.

This was a risky business because stray onlookers were apt to follow you home to gate-crash the party. So Pat, in a simple stroke of genius, put paid to all the problems by taking up beer and wine making. Suddenly the house and out buildings were full of gallon jars with corks and tubes in them, and bubbling gaseous noises and aromas issued from every corner of our terraced house. Some of the rooms looked like Jodrell Bank, some like a scene from the *Quatermass Experiment*. Suddenly we and our neighbours and friends became experts in parsley and carrot and elderberry wines. 'A spiteful little tang this one has.' We even got to the stage of aerating the stuff and convincing ourselves it was as good as champagne.

But the beer was the thing. Well, the beer was the killer. Miles over-proof and very more-ish, it was the spark that lit up many a good night in. No pain felt, no risk of a drunken drive home, no distance to fall when enough was enough. Fine for the residents of Hornby Road, Bootle. But what of those who travelled to visit? Not to beat about the bush – what about Father X? In our staunchly Catholic area of Liverpool in the 1940s, '50s and '60s, the link between church and home was forged in steel. All revolved around parish doings, and the clergy took a genuine and almost daily interest in all the families' welfare. So much so that there was a ritual of visits by one curate or another every Friday night, for a chat, advice, even monetary help. And so it came to pass that Father X arrived to visit at 6.30 pm one Friday and was offered the usual tea and biscuits 'Or, if you like, a drop of this beer Pat's brewed.'

'Go on, I'll give it a go,' said the reverend father. I remember those words exactly: it was the last lucid sentence he said that evening. After about five pints of the stuff and derogatory comments like: 'After a while it starts to taste watery', the good father attempted to leave. Big mistake. There's a saying in Liverpool pubs that, when drinking, 'You must keep a careful eye on the back legs. If they go you're dead'. Well, the reverend's legs, back and front, had gone AWOL and he was as stranded as any beached whale. What to do? No telephone in the house. Vandalised telephone in the street. Nothing for it than for me to cycle round to the church for assistance. I actually went to the presbytery to call out a priest to minister to Father X.

Guinness book of records stuff if only we'd dared tell the tale.

So imagine to yourself how potent Pat's brew must have been to knock over a fairly seasoned imbiber. And then picture its effect on a youngster – young Stephen. As little boys will, he let curiosity get the better of him when he found the latest batch of 'the stuff' gently fermenting in an enamel bucket, and decided to test drive a cup full. He was through that and into another when we caught him. Little knowing what the after effects might be (he seemed perfectly OK at the time), we allowed my mother to take him on a promised trip to Liverpool. What a day that turned out to be. Mother returned three hours later (and an hour overdue) red faced with exertion and temper to explain the unusual behaviour of 'little Stephen'. It seems 'the stuff' hadn't taken effect for about an hour, but then – Bingo! Her sweet little grandchild became Conan the Barbarian. He refused to go to this shop, and demanded to go to that shop. He lay down on a zebra crossing, blocking traffic, and screaming when picked up. He demanded to go to the loo every other minute, and at intervals would break into hysterical laughter. 'He was just like a drunken man,' said my mother. 'What do you think's the matter with him?' To tell the truth, all I could think was, 'I wonder if Father X kicked up like this after we got him home?'

It was about this time that things started to look up for us generally. On the one hand I received a graded post at work, which meant extra money, and on the other the club scene was booming and so was my reputation. Amazingly, I had chosen the avenue of clean, uncontroversial comedy and found myself the only exponent in my neck of the woods. Consequently I was regularly chosen for mid-week shows at which local dignitaries or family audiences were to be entertained. 'Mr Clean' or 'the Pope', as I was known to other comics, was beginning to reap the rewards of an act full of a kind of gentle comedy in which racial, religious or political jokes had no place. Up went the demand – and up went the fees. So much so I was able to indulge in a major investment: yes, my first car. And what a car! The love of my life, the best I've ever owned. It was nothing less than a 1962 Ford Popular. Carpers might mock its sit-up-and-beg posture, or its rather small engine or its three gears, or its dented front and rear. Some might even deny that its interesting off-yellow colour blended well with the attractive rusty brown around the door sills and wheel arches. But above all it was MINE! It was MY CAR! Yes, RDJ 705 was my pride and joy. No one but no one, was going to drive this car but me. No one, do you hear? Eh? Oh, all right then. Maybe just the missus. And just in order to learn to drive. Yes, no problem – I'll teach her.

Little did I know that in life there is one rule that simply *must* be obeyed if harmony is what you seek. Never – and I mean do not *ever* – attempt to teach your wife how to drive a car, least of all your own car.

The very first time she got behind the wheel Pat said to me: 'Before we start, don't you dare make this thing move. We're not going anywhere till those pigeons clear off the street.'

Eventually I convinced her that the birds would move when they heard the car approach. Nonetheless she insisted on honking the horn. The noise attracted the interested attention of neighbours and bystanders, who were no doubt amused to watch the 'Yellow Peril' (my nickname for the car) processing up the road by a series of leaps and bounds as Pat's left foot trembled on the clutch pedal while her right pumped more 'bouncy petrol' through the accelerator.

'Take your foot off or change up,' I reasoned with her. She must have heard – my voice rang out with wonderful clarity above the screaming of the engine.

'Foot off what? Up where?' she enquired, taking her eyes off the road.

'Stop the car, stop the car. This is hopeless,' I bellowed,

to the delight of the ever-growing gallery of onlookers.

'Shut up. What do *you* know?' said my beloved as she stalled the car, stepped out, slammed the door and stomped home. Twenty attempts to restart the machine, one flat battery, and a push start by weeping neighbours later, I sputtered home, almost noiselessly entered the kitchen, brewed a strong tea and began a conversation with Pat on a totally different, obscure topic. Not once then, nor for years later, did we refer to the day's events and never again have I remarked on her driving skills.

Still, the car gave us much more freedom of movement, and the chance for me to appear nightly in clubs even as far away as Yorkshire and the Midlands. Usually if the journey was $2\frac{1}{2}$ hours or less I would drive home at night to be with Pat and the family. Mostly all my children saw of me was a sleeping figure, but at least I was there. And the money was good. We bought things we'd only dreamed of before. A new gas cooker, for a start. Forty quids-worth, dammit. Beautiful to look at, hysterical to watch being installed. Albert and his young assistant Shane came from the Gas Board to do the necessaries.

'I used to be on the water till me eyes went,' said Albert in a tone that chilled the blood. 'Now I'm on gas 'cos I can still smell leaks.' This made me not a happy chappy, but he seemed to be doing all the right things, and I was going to have the work checked out later anyway. Shane, however, engendered a certain unease. 'Shane! Shane!' cried Albert. 'Put that Woodbine out and get me the wrench. You know, the long hooky-looking thing.' (Well, you have to admire a man who knows all the technical terms.)

'Arr aye, Albert. Give us a break will yer?'

'Listen, son,' said the oracle of the gas world. 'You don't know what hard graft is. When I was installing pipes in building sites in the old days they used to give us 15 ft of pipe start, then turn the water on and we'd be working ahead of the flow!'

This was a period of growing prosperity for the O'Connor clan, and so we added a fourth – Helen Rebecca. Now we were referred to as the Von Trapps and found it difficult to visit friends for fear of swamping their seating arrangements. The good thing was that as the fame grew, so did the children's ability to ride with it. No sudden overnight success, which must be like a pools win, leaving family and friends staggered and unable to decide how to react. No, this was a gradual process. There is a dish in Liverpool, a kind of stew called Scouse. 'You don't cook Scouse – it just accumulates.' Basically a pot of stew is kept on the simmer and any foodstuffs left over from meals are thrown into it until it becomes a meal itself. So my act became a pan of Scouse, additions being made daily and the strength of it growing to the point that I became a minor celebrity on Merseyside. Radio shows invited me to give opinions on world affairs, sport – anything that could be lightened by a one-line gag. Garden fetes and charity bazaars requested my presence to cut ribbons and 'say a few words – not more than forty minutes'. Even stores asked me to perform opening ceremonies and newspapers did in-depth interviews to try to learn the secret of my modest success. 'What makes you do it? Lust for the big time? Desire for recognition?' Money, the honest answer, never satisfied them. But sometimes pride came into it, too.

A local record store was opening a new branch and asked me to perform the rite. As I had a new comedy LP out on release, I was delighted to do so. Whilst I was 'circulating' and chatting to guests, a journalist questioned five-year-old Frances O'Connor:

'What's it like to have a famous daddy?'

'I don't know because I've never had an ordinary one,' was the wide-eyed reply. It's moments like this that do wonders for the ego.

I shan't have a great deal to say about my comedy or musical records because, like everyone else, I detest listening to my own voice being replayed. Nor can I bear to watch my appearances on TV – this, no doubt, something to do with the insecurity of a comedian. In the early days I would go into the gents' toilets and lock myself into a closet listening to the comments of my club audience:

'Funny? Nay, lad, but he's harmless.'

'Wouldn't pay him in washers.'

'I've seen some tripe in my time ...'

Ouch! But gradually, I realised this was a counter productive exercise. And nowadays I refuse to read (or believe) reviews of my shows – unless of course they're complimentary! But please allow me to dwell for a second on the story of my first LP.

Called *The Tom O'Connor Show*, it featured three musical acts including Ernie Mack's band, the Saturated Seven, and thirty minutes of my broadest Liverpool jokes in an even broader Liverpool accent. Boots the Chemist decided to help me launch the disc and put on a grand display in their main store. Every window was plastered with record covers, and huge posters blaring 'TOM O'CONNOR THIS WAY' led the populace to a corner cash desk where I stood proudly, pen in hand, to sign their purchases.

BB – Before Beadle – I thought I was witnessing a huge send up when a pimply, leather-clad youth swaggered up to me and said:

'Have you got Gary Glitter's latest LP?' I could tell by his eyes that he was sincere – he truly didn't know me from a hole in the wall.

'Yes, we have,' I muttered through clenched teeth. 'They're going for nothing – more than they're worth, I reckon!'

With that, I placed one of my records in a Gary Glitter cover and wrapped it up as neatly as my trembling hands could manage.

Just wait till he gets it home and plays it to his mates, I thought maliciously. Then a voice in my head said: Maybe they won't know the difference.

Maybe so. Maybe I'm now a cult figure in their circle.

I can picture the real G Glitter coming on TV and these misguided folk saying: 'That's not him – we've got the real thing on this record here.'

Oh, and one last word on that fated LP. It involves a sea cruise and Pat's supreme optimism. Who could resist the agent's offer? A family holiday at sea, a few bob spending money and all I had to do was three shows to the same audience aboard the ship. Hold me back! What an offer! So it was that the 'Von Trapps' boarded MV *Ithaca*, a Greek ship unique, I think, in the history of cruising. She could actually pitch and roll at the same time and could make the toughest of stomachs queasy. Still it was great to treat the youngsters to the fun aboard. Table tennis suited Stephen, although he spent most of the day chasing the ball around the deck. Helen and Frances enjoyed the junior club and entered the fancy dress contest, Frances as a Pixie and Helen, wearing every stitch of clothing we could put on her, was an Irish streaker. Anne haunted the disco, the dance classes and anywhere where there was music. Pat and I relaxed and made the most of the break from the treadmill at home. Also, we waited with trepidation for my big moment. Pat had decided to take copies of my record for sale to the passengers. Surely they would all want a copy? All seven hundred of them. Some might want two copies, who knows. What a mistake in human assessment that was. On the last night, following a storming cabaret spot, we opened shop and sold *two* LPs – and one of them was to the bandleader. This left me six hundred and ninety-eight copies to take home. Have you any idea how heavy they can be? And how much space they take up?

At Manchester airport our plane lurched along the taxi way with my trunk of LPs canting the whole thing sideways. Two handedly I dragged the overweight box through customs hoping not to be stopped. But I was not to be so lucky.

'What's in this?' enquired the sharp-eyed customs man. 'Something heavy?' (proving his wits to be just as sharp).

'Records.'

'Eh?'

'Records.'

'Oh, you're a disc jockey are you?'

'Er, no.'

'Strange. Open it up.'

Five minutes and as many padlocks later I flung open the lid and he was confronted by my unsold stock.

'Hm!' he mused. 'These are all the same.'

'I know.'

'And they're all of you.'

'Er. Yes, that's right.'

'Hm. OK, off you go,' he sighed resignedly as he scribbled a chalk mark on the lid. And as I slowly dragged the chest towards the exit gate he shouted in my direction: 'Big Head!'

Home from the sea and soon it was to be home from home. A move from Bootle and my roots and a step up in the accommodation stakes: a detached house in Formby – out in the country (well, sort of) and plenty of fresh air away from factory chimneys. A place of green for the children to run – a dream I'd had since I was their age. No leaky roofs, no cracked walls or ceilings, no hardened films of paint on the woodwork. Everything brand new to go with the house. £5,000 and worth every penny. We naturally had to have a new car. I found my dream in a small garage in Crosby – a brand new Morris 1000 Traveller all shiny and smelling of 'just finished'.

Super little car the Morris, and I needed her for the two dozen or so trips I made carrying Pat's wine and beer-making jars and pipes. I dreaded what the neighbours might think of us: Hippies hooked on the devil's brew. Shouldn't be allowed. Call the police. Actually, the reaction was totally different – more in the way of: 'Oh, boy – more plonkies like us!'

9

In thirty odd years of marriage Pat and I have lived in several houses, but 37 Deansgate Lane, Formby, was unique. It was our only brand-new house, the first with a front garden and, wonder of wonders, it had a huge back lawn – too much for the hand mower which was all we could afford. I remember the first day we moved in: Christmas Eve 1967. We had no gas, no electricity and no heating because of a mix up with the builders. Three children scampering round a house cluttered with packing cases. In desperation I screamed:

'Come on, all of you – out in the back yard!' (A sure sign of where we'd come from.)

Just then a van pulled up at the gate:

'Pat – it's the breadman,' I called.

'Baker here!' cried the man, establishing beyond doubt that we'd moved just a little up-market.

Still, it was a good house for us; room to spread and to build extensions. Room to relax and concentrate on the business of being funny. It was still a tight time money-wise and I often reminded myself of the old joke:

Customer: How much is this new TV on hire purchase?
Shopkeeper: Well, sir, you pay £5 now and then nothing for six months.

Customer: Who's been talking about me? It's all lies!

Yes there were times when bills were paid slowly, there were times when they had to go into the shuffle. You know the story? Well, the firm write a threatening letter to a householder regarding his late payments and he gets the credit controller on the phone saying:

'I can't pay all my bills, all the time. So what I do is, every month I get all the important ones together, shuffle them up and pay the top three. If you keep pestering me yours won't even go into the shuffle.'

Times weren't always that hard, and in some ways they got easier. There were more mid-week engagements coming in and the fees gradually went up. More, and more varied, clubs, and even theatres began booking me. Soon our family could relax and enjoy some of the good things in life – like holidays. Holidays? Well, short breaks anyway. It had to be my family, resident in Formby, who would decide to go on a week's holiday to Pontin's Ainsdale – three miles down the road! Still, it was a great place for the kids, live entertainment, blue coats to keep them amused (and tire them out) and talent competitions. Oh dear, yes, the talent competitions. The one and only time I've been physically sick back stage from nerves. No, not for me, but for Anne, our eldest girl. She'd decided to enter the talent finals singing and playing the guitar. I'd tried to help by re-stringing the guitar, but the new strings had stretched and de-tuned it. She went on stage without a qualm, while I sat quivering in the dressing room. She came second and I lost a stone in sweat.

Still, it was a start for the family in the world of footlights, spotlights, and microphones and happy faces. Gradually, all the offspring would go the way of Anne and enter the business, albeit from different directions. Meantime, dad pressed on spreading the act nationwide and waiting for that elusive 'break' – the one shot on

TV that turns a no-hoper into a champ; the one shot that means instant and lasting stardom. The one shot that, when it does come, is usually so late that you hardly notice its arrival.

Meantime, it was Sheffield for me. Sheffield was one of the hot spots of the club scene. At the time there was plenty of work for miners and steelmen, and plenty of scope for comics to entertain them. The city was about $2\frac{1}{2}$ hours' drive from our home, over Snake Pass in the Pennines. I was offered £12 a night, but, more importantly, £100 per week if I could fill in all the dates. One week I did Sunday noon and seven nights in different clubs. Boy, oh boy, I couldn't wait to get here. The brain was in over-think. Why not save a load of petrol money by staying in digs? £12 per week B and B, that would leave seventy odd quid when the commission was paid – enough to buy a power mower plus lots of other goodies for the house.

Suitably organised I arrived at the St Francis working men's club (I've changed the name – you'll see why) to do the Sunday noon show. It was a huge room full of men – about 800 of them. There were three acts on the bill. A tenor who was the greatest and most popular in Yorkshire (or so he told me) and a 'girl' singer who was 40-plus but with a resemblance to Marlene Dietrich (or so she told me).

I had the choice of doing one show at noon and two at night or vice versa. I opted for one show at noon on the grounds that there was less chance of dying and being sacked.

NB – an important rule of showbusiness. Always get off before you're found out (or more realistically – found wanting!)

The 'popular' tenor went down like a kick in the groin and was sacked on the spot. The girl singer struggled through dimly recognisable attempts at 'Danny Boy' and 'Proud Mary', showed lots of leg, and lived to reappear that

evening. Somewhat to my surprise, my football and docker
stories struck home, while a few country numbers got them
at least humming, if not actually joining in. I suppose I
knew I'd cracked it when a chap approached the stage and
said:

'Hey, son. Tha' knows that box behind thee?' (motioning
towards my amplifier).

'Yee ... ss,' I stuttered.

'Is it supposed to be on fire?'

I turned round to see smoke billowing out of the amp.
So it was a credit to the act (I later thought) that until then
no-one had wanted to interrupt me by telling me about it.
On second thoughts, maybe that's what was keeping them
quiet. Worse still, maybe they hoped to see me go up in a
blue flash. Who knows? At all events I survived to reappear
that night after checking into my digs for lunch and an
hour's nod.

Surprise, surprise, guess who was staying at the same
guesthouse? The wannabee Marlene Dietrich. I offered her
a lift back from the theatre because she knew the way, and
in the twenty-minute car ride she explained her off-stage
interests, which included escorting men and posing for some
very explicit photographs. She had wads of these in her
handbag, each with her phone number scrawled on the
back. No, I never took one, and I resolved to give her a
wide berth. My resolution was strengthened after I'd talked
to a chap at the guesthouse, a newly promoted police
sergeant who was staying there for a week or so until his
family joined him from Hull.

'Watch that one,' warned 'the Bill', 'she wanders in the
night, you know.'

That, as they say, did it for me. That night I slept with a
chair under my door knob. The next day I checked out, and
spent the next six days commuting to and from home,
arriving shattered at each venue.

But things were getting better. I even tried a spell of full-time showbiz work, giving teaching a couple of terms' rest while I toured major venues all over Britain. I always seemed to go down pretty well – but I never made that elusive breakthrough. What I did not realise at the time was that all this graft, this honing of my technique and material, would serve me well when (if!) the big break came along. Experiences undergone, ordeals suffered, routines tempered in the fire of rough clubs and drunken audiences – all would be invaluable when the time came. Meantime, soldier on O'Connor, take the plaudits and brickbats, always find some small reason to keep going. Like the golfer who hits only one good shot a round, keep coming back for more.

Everything that can go wrong does go wrong and generally it's down to you, O comic. On the other hand, you can't really be blamed if the venue falls down. *Falls down?* Yes, honest to God – I was there. My big moment had arrived, or so my addled brain told me. I had been engaged to open a brand new club in Lancashire. Constructed in pre-cast concrete slabs, the whole structure was supported by six pillars into which the slabs were grooved, then covered with mortar and plaster. It only took thirty days to erect £150,000 worth of entertainment luxury – so they got a £12 comic to open the proceedings.

Looking back, it was a wonderful feeling driving into the four-acre tarmac-ed car park – surely enough space for the entire county to leave their vehicles? In past the commissionaire I strode, deposited my guitar backstage and began wrapping myself around a pint of best bitter. Meanwhile, a coachload of senior citizens had arrived outside and, as they de-bussed, the driver climbed down to join them.

'Oi! Where do you think you're going?' asked the jobsworth commissionaire.

'In for a bevvy,' answered driver Jack.

'Well you can't leave that bus there, mate. It's blocking car park!'

'Eh? What? How can it block four bleeding acres, you boss-eyed wazzock?' (or words to that effect).

'Look, I only know what I know (sounds reasonable). You've got to move the damn thing and pronto.'

In a fury, driver Jack leapt back into his cab, slammed the fifty-seater into reverse by mistake and backed into the club at a great rate of knots.

Crump (as he hit a main pillar). *Graunch* (as the pillar snapped in the middle). *Tinkle, tinkle* (as the plaster and mortar spattered from ceiling into punters' beer glasses).

'Flipping heck,' screamed the club secretary. 'Let's get out of here.'

So slowly, I mean like snail-pace, we picked up our belongings and drinks, and wandered into the car park to watch awstruck as the entire club crumpled inwards. What a sight! Fastest ever *con*struction followed by fastest ever *de*struction – a double header for the record books.

All this left me with two thoughts: first, would I ever get paid, or just re-booked in the hope that they would rebuild the place? (Actually, I got half the fee; the site was abandoned.) Second, what ever became of driver Jack? I mean, picture his conversation with the boss of the coach firm.

'I've had a bit of a knock, Jim.'

'Oh, really – any damage?'

'Well, no, just a dent in the back bumper.'

'Any third party problem?'

'Well, Jim, this £150,000 club fell down.'

Not only comics have nightmare days at work. But at least it made a good story to trade with other entertainers over a late-night jar. It reminds me of the tale that everybody relates but nobody can pin down to a particular venue. The story goes that the club had built a brewery-subsidised extension, and had a Wednesday beanfeast for the committee only. During the course of the booze up, the steward realised that the bar was light by about six cases of lager. What to be done? A thief already? Who could it be? 'OK. So be it, lads,' said the club chairman. 'Swallow the cost through petty cash, and let's instal a proper alarm and padlock system so it doesn't happen again.' So Saturday night came, the alarm system was installed and the official opening began with the mayor cutting a tape and leading the members to the concert room, where they were to be greeted by a fanfare on the new £15,000 organ. On folding back the leather organ cover, the steward found he was staring down at six cases of lager! The thieves on Wednesday had certainly got more than could be swallowed by petty cash!

Whilst tales like this were circulating and I was embellishing them where I could, I was gradually attracting more and more notice. Most important, interest was being shown by the media. First there were newspaper stories of teacher-turned-funny-man. Then I started appearing on radio chat shows, discussion programmes and even a live phone-in. Boy, was the phone-in fraught with danger! Well-spoken, apparently genteel ladies would launch into the most amazingly rude stories, which failed to scorch the airwaves only because I cut them off, pretending there was static on the line. (There was no fail-safe mechanism in those days, now they put the programme out five seconds after it is actually recorded, giving leeway to sever communications when necessary.)

From radio to television – and suddenly my big break seemed at hand. I was invited to appear on *The Comedians*. Already a well established ratings leader, this show featured several comics on the same show, each telling gags on set subjects, with the director cutting from one to the other. Very watchable stuff, and the making of Charlie Williams, Ken Goodwin, Frank Carson, and Bernard Manning – but not me! I wasn't a gag man, only a patter merchant, a one-line hitter and not really what the show wanted. Pity. Too bad. Hard luck. Thank you and goodnight.

Still, it was a try and it *was* television, and it *did* raise my sights. I also realised how much talent there was in the comedy world, how many jokes I hadn't heard, how many things I had still to learn. One of the things I learnt was that despite my own high opinion of it, my act was not good enough to get me to the top. More work, more travel, more highs and an awful lot more lows would be endured before I would be ready. In hindsight it was a godsend the big break hadn't come so soon – I wouldn't have lasted two minutes in the cauldron of the big time.

So I waited, I worked, I watched, I learned, I practised – boy, did I practise! Two clubs a night, sometimes three, children's parties, after-dinner speeches – anything to stretch myself and my repertoire. New lines, new routines, new sketches – all tried out without rehearsal. It left agents demented with worry. My methodical brain decided that the best way to try out new material was to insert it at the top of the act. Any competent comedian can get a laugh with any gag after half an hour on stage, but to get laughs early on needs good material. So, the new stuff went in early and if it worked, it stayed in. The fear factor – fear of failure – is responsible for the success of nearly all my routines. It's amazing what you can do when your whole future depends on it.

Year by year the quality of my act improved, and with it my confidence grew. Allinson's theatre club booked me for several weeks as compère. It was great training, and gave me an invaluable insight into the technique of presenting acts on stage. Details like where to leave the microphone stand, and where to enter and exit without bumping into the artiste. But also how to coax, cajole, bully, or molly-coddle the performers so they would give of their best. And, crucially, how to set up an audience so that the act could knock them down – the hallmark of the best compères. On the face of it, this might seem rather a thankless role: working hard so others get the credit. But it doesn't work like that. The good compères get noticed by those who know – those who, in the long run, have the say as to your future. All this goes on year after year, a word here, a recommendation there, a good press write up, a small mention on radio, and suddenly – bingo! When you're least expecting it, into town rides the man on the white horse. Well, in my case the man with white hair – none other than Hughie Green. Let me tell you like it was.

By 1974 I was topping the bill in every nightspot in Liverpool; I could even stipulate the time at which I would go on. It was busy, busy, with no time to think: get on, do an hour, get off, get out. One of these venues was a beautiful nightspot called Russells Club – a place for the more discriminating clubgoer and a club that deserved to do better. I remember the owner, Norman Baker, presenting me with a trophy after fifty consecutive appearances, accompanying it with a Winston Churchill crown coin on which was inscribed the club motto: 'Never was so much owed'.

Monday nights Norman and I had a deal. I could appear at any time between 8 and midnight. I would appear for an hour and earn £30: fair price, fair deal, and good rehearsal time for me. Crowds used to come along to give an opinion on the new stuff. It was rather like the marking system at ice-skating events.

Every Monday was like every other, give or take an hour between start times, and every Monday was fun. No problems, no stress: just enjoy the limelight and earn a crust. My special Monday felt like every other. No trumpets, no flashing lights, no standing ovation. Just a roomful of friendly and eager faces. Except that on this night the crowd included Hughie and his team, seated out of my vision and enjoying a late-night meal. They'd earned every crumb of it by auditioning over 300 acts that day: spoons-players, singers, poets, blue comedians, fire-eaters – you name it, they'd sat through it! What they didn't need was another 'turn', especially one on for an hour. Still, they were patient, they listened, and, wonder of wonders, they liked me.

'You were on over an hour, didn't swear, didn't pick on anybody – and, son, it was funny.' The great man had spoken. I had unwittingly passed the audition of my life. Would I like to be on his show? *Would I?* 'Can we do it tonight while the gags are still warm?'

'Not tonight, but soon,' he promised.

Opportunity Knocks was a Monday night show that was never out of the ratings top 10. It was recorded as 'live' in the afternoon and was a classic in presenting variety acts. Each week would see a varied bill – music, comedy, speciality acts, dancers – and it was very apparent that Hughie's hand guided the whole affair. Could we try the entrance a different way? Could the girl be dressed in brighter colours? Would it help if the comic made a joke about him? Every effort was put into presenting acts at their best – a godsend to nervous wannabees waiting their turn.

For me the props team built a small platform 9 in high so that when I talked to the studio audience, my eye level was just right for the cameras. My old headmaster, Steve Brown, introduced me and somehow I stumbled on and rattled through my holiday routine, finishing with a thought for the day: 'The greatest gift you can give a child is time. The greatest gift you can give a comedian is time. Thanks for giving this comedian a little of your time.'

Somehow, this formula worked on TV and, wonder of wonders, I won the studio vote and the viewers' postcard vote. So my fears were ended. Surely the biggest dread of a fairly successful act is to fail at a major hurdle in their career. But to win *Opportunity Knocks*, the first comic to do so, was like winning the pools, or having your own TV series.

The winner of each show came back the following week. And, wouldn't you know it, I won again and again. Three wins and the all-winners show meant I'd virtually had my 'own' series for five weeks. Now the work flooded in. Clubs, theatres, radio, TV – all sorts of doors opened and things began to look up. Hughie Green, ever protective of his discoveries, took a firm interest in my doings and was a fund of good advice. We would meet on a regular basis while on the circuit. Often I'd attend his auditions and give the 'up-and-comings' an idea of the heights they could reach if they worked hard and listened to good advice.

We had a great summer season on the Isle of Man in 1975 – Hughie's show at the Villa Marina, and me and my homegrown variety bill at the Gaiety Theatre. It was Pat's idea that we took our own theatre show to the booming island, and in retrospect it was as simple as could be. We approached acts we'd worked with on the circuit: Sheila and Clyde, a brilliant vocal duo; Blanche Finley and the Prophets, a group of university bods with a fine lead vocalist; magic and mystery from a young Blackpool couple; and four girl dancers from our children's ballet school. The show was an instant hit and we packed out every performance – despite the forged £5 scare I mentioned earlier. On Sundays we featured Joseph Karma, a very funny hypnotist who did the whole show on his own and helped us have a season to remember. There must be people who remember that show, but I wonder if they were there on the Christmas party night. We'd decided, for reasons I know not, to have a Christmas party on August Bank Holiday Sunday night. We'd ordered a couple of turkeys, we'd brought a tree and decorations – even crackers. Back stage we had a huge oven and during Joe Karma's show we were basting the birds and preparing the punch. On stage Joe was making the most of things:

'Imagine you're all at home. It's Christmas time and the family are due to call any minute.'

There sat an audience, some entranced, some just happy to humour the old hypnotist. 'If you close your eyes, you can smell the turkey cooking in the kitchen.'

A couple of thousand sniffs later the whole audience was saying: 'He's right, you know! You *can* smell turkey! Boy, what an act!'

A good summer, 1975 – and even better was to come. It was a tribute to the Hughie Green 'after-sales service' and then the 'big break' – the leap into the big time. Of course, national interest was always high in Hughie's contest winners. But usually they were singers, who duly followed up with a hit record. Think of Peters and Lee, Mary Hopkin, Millican and Nesbitt, Lena Zavaroni – the formula was tried and trusted. But what about comedians?

I was first off the jig as a comedian winner, so what to do? Hughie knew. In the series following my debut he found he had an all-winners show with no comic. Would I consider doing a guest spot? Is the Pope a catholic? I was there like a shot and I'd prepared the act, honed to the exact second, even allowing for laughs (please God there'd be laughs). A new suit had been made to measure – velvet, no less – and Pat had bought me not one but two pairs of patent leather (well, to be honest, plastic) shoes. All was packed and off I set for my date with destiny. But, like many momentous occasions, it came not with a blare of trumpets but with a normal, run-of-the-mill, showbusiness crisis. To begin with, Pat had packed two left shoes in my bag and, try as I might to walk in them, the whole thing was doomed to failure. Would the viewing audience notice if I went on in socks? No need to worry. My face, my show, my future was saved by that wonderful man Benny Hill, who kindly lent me a pair of black shoes.

Clad in this magic footwear I went on as a guest and delivered a very crisp three-minute spiel. Applause. Thanks from Hughie. Exit to dressing room to return shoes, and pack for home. But wait! I was stopped in the corridor by a very nice chap. I was still buzzing from my performance and I had to concentrate hard on his words. He seemed to be saying things like 'New game show ... mathematics and music mixture ... compère....'

At this point Billy Uke Scott, my manager, appeared and explained that the man was Philip Jones, head of light entertainment at Thames TV. He had an idea for a massive variety show featuring stars, dancers and a game show called 'Name That Tune' – a musical quiz with a mathematical bent – ideal for a teacher qualified in sums and drums (my ex-pupils' slang for maths and music).

Would I do a dummy run-type show? I would! Would I like Thames TV to find me writers? Would I like Dick Hills and Spike Mullins? All this time, through all the questions, I was waiting for Candid Camera to rear its head, but it didn't. Instead, the dream started to come true.

Try to picture all the wishes you would personally make if a leprechaun appeared. Now imagine that they all came true. What would you do? Leap up and down? Scream with joy? No. You'd do what I did. You'd stand there, mouth open, eyes rolling and nodding your head to everything. It's the best thing to do, just in case it is all a dream and any sudden movement will wake you up.

This was it. Out of nowhere had come the moment. Would the man be up to the job? He would if he listened to those around him. He would if he did as he was told. He would if he did what I did – nodded the head, rolled the eyes and then got stuck into the serious job of being funny.

10

If the truth were known, behind every successful comedian there is at least one or, if he's lucky, two, good writers. I was lucky. I had two of the best. Dick Hills, a man who'd been there and back with the finest – Morecambe and Wise, Tommy Cooper, Dave King – was Mr Motivator. 'Listen, son,' he'd say, 'tell the gag to the studio audience but the *tag* to the camera. Use the camera, it's only a prop.' How right he was. Spike Mullins, a quietly spoken genius, took everything and stored it in the memory bank for life. Spike got right into my style and reeled out an endless stream of great one liners:

'When I was small you could always tell the posh kids – they wouldn't take a sweet off you if it had been in your mouth.'

'Most of their windows had glass.'

'They collected bonfire wood with their gloves on.'

We three spent many hours putting the world of comedy to rights and trying to squeeze the best out of any gag situation. Spike would take notes copiously as we drank a few beers and smoked a few dozen fags. Sadly his notes were in his own brand of long and short-hand and many's a time his wife Mary would ring me up the morning after and try to make some sense of what he'd written:

'It's something about a cat, a ladder and I *think* the Duke of Edinburgh – but honestly it's really just a demented scrawl!'

That was about par for the course. We always began with pages of rot and gradually kicked it around into a workable shape. In this we were lucky to be guided (no, ordered about) by a very fine producer/director William G Stewart – now host of *15 to One*. Without doubt the finest TV director I ever worked with, he was also a great fan of comedy and comedians and he had the gift of knowing what was, and was not, the best way to present a gag.

William, Dick, Spike and I welded a very strong format for a half-hour series and were able to knock out six in a row – each of which reached the ratings top 10. And now I was ready to face the big one: the true test of the funny man, the vehicle that could make or break in one evening – the big television show. Presenting other acts on TV and ensuring they appeared at their best, even to your own detriment – surely I'd been here before? Allinson's club years before – same procedure just a smaller audience. Ah, but that was the rub. The audience this time would be 15 million plus! Plenty of witnesses if you died a death!

I got lucky. To begin with, the choice of producer was inspired: Royston Mayo. Through Roy the venue was ideal: Lakeside Country Club at Frimley. The showbill was packed with talent: Des O'Connor, Georgie Fame, Roger de Courcey, dancers and a big band. You'll remember the year, if not the show: it was the very hot, parched summer of '76, with temperatures forever in the 90s and everyone suffering from sunburn and flaking skin. At the Lakeside, sales of ice-cold lager hit an all-time high, as I faced an audience of 2000 plus in a baking hot club. Despite the oppressive conditions the punters were magnificent and the show went like a dream. My patter went well and all the links worked. Roger de Courcey made me howl with his cross-chat with Nookie. The bear had upset some ladies who wouldn't stop nattering. Unfortunately the ladies were accompanied by half a dozen heavies – Schwartzeneggers all – who took umbrage at the dummy's putdowns. Roger knew how to cope:

'Now, Nookie, that's very naughty,' admonished Roger. 'You've upset all those nice gentlemen.'

'Doesn't worry me, mate,' snapped Nookie. 'It ain't me they're going to hit.'

Fight prevented, laughs all round, sigh of relief from the compère. Congratulations from Roy Mayo; another brick in the wall. 'See you at the studios next week.' I was in!

So there at least was proof of my ability to host a variety show. But what about the other major factor, the game show? If there was a quiz for which I was ready made it was 'Name That Tune'. An American format, reputedly owned by ex-President Gerald Ford, it had the lot. Plenty of popular music, big prizes, terrific pace – a surefire winner from the off – at least in the States. But would it transplant to Britain? Could it be adapted to suit the slightly more reserved Brits over here? Well, we'd give it a damned good try!

When I first watched a complete American tape, featuring a host called Tom Kennedy (a Clark Kent lookalike), I thought: 'My God, they'll never accept that – never!' The whole studio audience were potential contestants and had come dressed to attract the attention of the producer. People were dressed as penguins, giraffes, hula dancers, clowns, virtually every type of costume that could be hired. They jumped up and down in the studio, screaming and dancing at the command of the warm up man. It was bedlam. Eventually two were chosen and the bounds of taste were further stretched as the cameras picked up shots of their expectant families: widowed mother, a brother who'd lost an arm in Vietnam, children with mouths full of teeth braces and eyes gaping wonderingly. 'Mawkish' was the word that sprang to mind. And everything was accompanied by hooters, whistles and shrieks from the audience.

The contestants had to run to a board and rip off words to leave a tune title. More chaos. Then the money-tree feature saw an old lady, with what looked like an ice cream tray around her neck, snatching money off a Christmas tree while her opponent tried to guess the name of a tune. 'Dear God!' I thought. 'The game show from hell. Surely they're not expecting me to compère something like this?'

As if to read my mind, the researcher Jack Andrews said: 'Don't worry – it won't be anything like this. The basic show is what we're after. There'll be no noise, no panic – just fun.'

And fun it turned out to be. Lots of it – for us and for the hundreds of contestants who took part and, win or lose, had a good time. In one go, by selection of the right team, the best musicians, writers and researchers, we were lucky enough to produce two pilot shows that could have been transmitted, they were so good. On reflection, I realise that it was the work that went into these two pilots that formed the basis of my career as a game show host, which has spanned almost twenty years and eight different quizzes.

So how did it all gel? Well, the major credit must go to the producer Dennis Kirkland. A man later to find fame with Benny Hill and Freddie Starr, Dennis was my mentor, my confidant and my friend.

His basic, no-nonsense advice was: 'Get stuck in and be yourself, son, and you'll be fine. No worries – just let it flow.'

Oh, Dennis, if you only knew the worries I had! Especially the fear of getting the slightest thing wrong – despite the safety net of video recording. In my effort to repay the trust and confidence placed in me, I rehearsed that quiz till it came out of my ears. God help any visitors to our house. They were immediately enlisted as stand-in contestants, as I went over and over the show, round by round, looking for any small item I might have missed. By the time the recordings were made I knew every tune off by heart – there was nothing you could ask me that I didn't know the answer to. Nothing could go wrong. I was ready to 'let it flow'.

Ah, but you see I and the several hundred others on the team had not prepared ourselves for a little lady called Doris, our first female contestant, who was about to wipe the smiles off all of our faces. Because we were launching a brand new show – and in 1976 there were not so many game shows on TV and they were all a source of wonder to the contestants – we realised that our two players were likely to be nervous. Just how nervous we weren't to find out until just before the off. We'd chatted to them, had lunch and joined them in a glass of wine hoping that this would be enough to calm them down, but we were wrong. As the minutes ticked by to recording time they became more and more edgy and physically drawn.

'They're going to faint if we're not careful,' said Dennis. 'Let's scrap any rehearsal and just go for a take.'

'But they haven't even seen the equipment,' I said, horrified.

'Don't worry – go with the flow.'

So the flow was gone with. Two lovely folk, both good at music, but totally ignorant of the rules and procedures of 'Name That Tune', strode on to the set to play. Those who recall the show will remember that there was a money wheel involved. The host would spin it and the point where it stopped indicated the amount that could be won by naming a specific tune. The wheel was attached to a musical device which played a tune as the wheel revolved.

The first time I spun the wheel, a sound like an ambulance siren emerged. That is to say, it sounded like an ambulance siren to everyone except Doris, whose face lit up: ' "Somewhere Over the Rainbow",' she cried triumphantly.

'We haven't played the tune yet,' I explained.

'That wheel's playing "Somewhere Over the Rainbow",' Doris insisted. And suddenly we realised she might have a point – it *did* sound, ever so slightly, like 'Over the Rainbow'.

So stop the show, reload the tape, and this time, Mr
Compère, please explain the thing *fully* before spinning the
wheel. Jack Andrews assured me the situation would never
happen again. Good old Jack.

The plan was quite simple. Jack would sit in the front
row of the audience with a book of rules on his knee, and
earphones on his head. In the event of a query, I would
refer to him and, off-camera, he would give me the 'thumbs
up' for yes and 'thumbs down' for no.

So, as night follows day, the first show after the plan was
formed we ran into another problem. The contestant guessed
that the tune title was 'Pretty Woman', the Roy Orbison
hit. Now, strictly speaking, the correct answer was 'Oh
Pretty Woman'. Could we accept it? I looked at Jack for a
thumbs up or down and all I got was a shrug of the
shoulders! Just what I needed in a crisis. Oh, dear! Oh, my
goodness, how very unfortunate! was the general drift of
my comments. And so, back to the drawing board.

Plan two was foolproof, they said. It would take all the
worry out of my end of the job and plonk it squarely in the
court of the producer or his assistant. I would be fitted with
an earpiece – the latest in modern design. This meant having
the equivalent of a mouth of chewing gum wedged into the
right ear and a cable trailed down the back of the jacket,
down the trouser legs and, as far as I knew, out into the
car park. Seven years that appliance was in my ear – seven
years and not once did I hear 'Hello', 'Goodbye', 'testing'
or anything else in my earpiece until the first time we played
the game with a car as first prize.

The format had changed somewhat. The big variety show
had been dropped and *Name That Tune* became a half-hour
programme in its own right, with flashing lights, plenty of
glitz and bigger prizes. The top attraction was won by
guessing the title of a mystery tune whilst locked in a box.
Simple enough. But the problem was that there was a
financial constraint on the prizes and so we were limited as

to which cars we could give away. There was an insistence on British makes so that whittled our choice down even further. About £5000 was our budget and on the first and second shows we were going to feature the same car. So the day came and as I entered the studio I beheld the gleaming vehicle highlighted by the very brightest of neon. Boy, the car looked a smasher. What make was it? 'The basic model Ford Fiesta,' I was assured. 'I don't think so,' I said. 'My daughter has one and it doesn't look like this one.' It turned out that we had the top spec 1.3 Ghia version of the Fiesta – at a price about seven hundred pounds above our financial ceiling! My God, what to do? There was no way the contestant could be seen to win a prize that was above the limit.

'We'll all be sacked,' moaned a member of the production team, helpfully. 'We've had it.'

Nothing for it but to get out the prayer mat and humbly beseech the Almighty to give us a tune that would be impossible to name.

Imagine the stress, worry, panic, and prayers that greeted the star prize round. The contestant entered the glass booth – not soundproof, but it looked it. Earphones on his head – we were set to play 20 seconds of the mystery tune, and then allow 10 seconds for the title to be guessed.

The title was 'Wave', a difficult tune to guess because it was not a song and so there were no words to help.

'Waves,' said our brave contestant.

'Well,' said I, 'the rules state that if what you say includes the answer then I can accept it. The word "waves" includes the word "Wave", so you've won the car.'

'No he hasn't, no he hasn't, no he hasn't,' screamed a voice in my earpiece. But no one had spoken to me for seven years, so I just ignored it.

'Come out of the box and let's look at this beautiful car,' I beamed.

'You give him that car and you're paying for it,' said a

desperate voice. My heart sank. But all was well. I gave him the car and I didn't pay for it. Thank you, Thames TV, for your understanding. And thank you, Lord, for helping your too-confident servant through another crisis.

So the die was cast, the quiz master was launched and my whole career was being steered towards the game-show host and away from the stand-up comedian. This was a period in which I inevitably lost some of my popularity on the club and cabaret circuit. It was great that millions of people enjoyed being entertained by my quiz shows on TV; but few of them had any idea that the compère could also make them laugh. So the attraction of Tom O'C as a talker was beginning to wane a little, and I wanted to put that right. A think-tank of family, management and friends came up with a brilliant solution: take the TV show to the public. Let the game show attract the audience and then hit them with the comedy while they were there. Simple – and a very, very good decision. One of the major turning points in my early years.

Sponsored by electronics giant Philips, we were able to give away TVs, radio cassette players, razors and many other prizes, and this attracted bookings far and wide. One particular holiday camp circuit booked the show for the entire summer. So now we had to groove in a fail-safe system so that the show worked every time.

'Remember,' we stressed to the holiday camp managers, 'we can't just give these prizes away. The competitors have got to know the answers.'

'So?'

'So why don't you audition the holidaymakers before we arrive. We'll give you a tape of 20 popular tunes. Let the audience write down the answers, and we'll mark the papers when we arrive.'

'Great idea, Tom. Gives us an extra activity for the Saturday night.'

So all the camps decided to play our tapes – well, all

except one. One of the northern centres came up with the masterstroke: to find the two people to play Name That Tune they would have an elimination waltz. Don't look at me like that – I don't know why, either. Just because your feet move doesn't guarantee your head works. Still, that was the camp's decision and we had to go along with it. So imagine you're on your holidays. It's Saturday night, you've just arrived and the band leader announces an elimination waltz. Obviously you'd dance with your husband or wife. So I ended up with a married couple as my pair of contestants.

'Wait a minute – these two are married,' objected the entertainment boss.

'Yes,' I said.

'That means all the prizes will go to one chalet.'

'Yes,' I said.

'The others will go mad if that comes out. There'll be skin and hair flying.' So then he had a brainwave (or possibly a brainstorm): 'You'll have to pretend they don't know each other!'

'Oh, wow – what fun,' I groaned.

The show began and I battered the holidaymakers with lively patter, topical and otherwise. The vibes were good and the whole show was slowly climbing to a peak. Then on came the two volunteers. Here were two lovely folk, married for thirty-five years and pretending to be strangers. All was well until we came to the Bid A Note round, which is based on guessing tunes from an obscure clue.

'I'll give you clues to the identity of certain famous tunes,' I told them. 'Then I'll ask you to bid against each other as to how many notes it will take you to name that tune. The highest bid is seven notes, the lowest bid is one note. Understand?' (Nods from both parties.)

So I read the clue and said to the lady: 'Start the bidding.'

'I'll name that tune in seven,' she said.

I turned to her husband-cum-stranger.

'I'll name it in eight,' he insisted. Laughter from the

audience. And then *she* said: 'Oh, let him name it or he'll sulk for the rest of the holidays.'

Mixed laughter and amazement, but at the end of it all a good story to put in the act.

Show after show, live or on TV, gradually honed the quizmaster element in me and firmed up my knowledge of all facets of game shows. Basically they are all the same and it's a matter of which way you conduct business within the boundaries of set rules. It becomes second nature to analyse the pros and cons of any show and come to a decision on format. It helped that we were forever changing the various rounds in our show to maintain interest. With all this basic groundwork under my belt, it was not long before there were other demands for my talent.

Channel 4 had come up with a show called *Password*, a word-association game which featured celebrities and punters in a quest for prizes. Would I like to host the first two series? Good news. But the slightly less good news was that we had to film the whole shebang in a week. Twenty-six shows in seven days! Admittedly we'd knocked off four *Name That Tunes* per day, but now we were dealing with many more people per show and were working to a much smaller budget.

The essence of *Password*, a game now hosted superbly by Gordon Burns, was to pass to your partner a word chosen at random by the compère. Only one-word clues were allowed, and the faster the word was guessed, the more points were awarded. An example would be:

Word: 'toothache'
Clue 1: 'neuralgia'
Clue 2: 'pain'
Clue 3: 'gum'

And so on until one or other side found the answer. The major drawback was that it could never be predicted which words were easy to guess or which track the clue givers would go down.

Just for a laugh, try passing the word 'ply' to a pal using only one word clues. Tricky, to say the least.

The Americans, bless their efficient hearts, had come up with a wondrous piece of apparatus which enabled the 'randomness' of words to be controlled. Cards could be fired along wires to a point under the host's desk, thus ballowing easier clue words to be selected if both sides had reached an impasse. This was better – and much quicker – than watching the compère ferreting through a box of cards on his desk to find an easy clue. Our problem was that the American machine cost about a quarter of a million quid, so it was outside our budget by about £249,999.50. So we adapted as only the British can. We would replace the magic wire appliance by human power – ever ready and in great supply. On our beautifully erected and garishly lit set we installed a stagehand under my desk with a box of words and an earpiece. (Oh, hell, I thought, not another earpiece!) There he lay, all six and a half feet of him, on a bean bag, and waited for instructions from the control box:

'Give him number 61.'
'Now give him 27.'

Imagine the set up. In a line we had a celebrity and a punter seated behind the desk with me stood up between the two teams. At given intervals I would drop my hand below desk-top level and a card was slapped into it. This system worked for most of the early recordings and enabled us to keep a steady flow going. Then, inexorably, Murphy's Law intervened. We came to the debut of a lovely actress who arrived smartly dressed in a very trendy jacket and a short skirt. Her partner was similarly clad and they sat down to play, which meant that their respective skirts rose to at least mid-thigh level. The game began with no hassle, and certainly no traumas, until suddenly our actress leaned down to discard her shoes and spotted our unwitting stagehand lying below. With a terrific squeal of indignant horror she and her partner leapt to their feet, knocking over the whole set and revealing our card man to the unsuspecting audience. Roars of laughter; stuttering apologies and frantic explanations all round – and a one-hour break whilst a 'modesty curtain' was erected across the desk to limit the stagehand's view.

Regrettably, when we returned to the business of recording I found it impossible to control the giggles. Twenty minutes it took me to calm down. Why? Because every time the hand came through the curtain all I could think of was Sooty in the nude! The things that go on behind the scenes of what looks like a normal easygoing programme!

Password led to other game shows, some disastrous, others ever memorable. Some had well-established formats; others had formats that still weren't right after thirty or forty shows! *Gambit* was one of my favourites for lots of reasons. I'd been a fan for those years when the brilliant Fred Dineage had hosted the show. Depending on both skill and chance, it was perhaps the most perfect quiz I ever hosted. Why it was taken off the network I'll never know. *Gambit* was based on the card game pontoon, or blackjack, and truly relied on the turn of a card and the choice of 'stick' or 'twist'. We offered some great prizes – TVs, freezers, videos, golf clubs, together with star prizes of cars, dining-room suites, caravans – even bars of silver! The format was rock solid, the pace was brisk to say the least and the only minor drawback (if you could call it that) was that the star prize could go at any time in the show. It meant that we didn't always build up to a last-minute climax, which I suppose is the accepted norm today. Rather, we would move briskly from round to round, stopping in mid-stream when necessary and inviting our couples to return 'tomorrow' – which in reality meant 20 minutes later, after we'd all changed clothes.

I loved *Gambit*. I loved the friendly atmosphere and the wholehearted support of the crew at Anglia TV. Everyone was a friend and everyone was prepared to work till dooms-day to ensure our success. I've been given much in my time: Anglia gave me everything. I hope I repaid just a little. My memories are of non-stop good times. Script conferences where a room full of clergy, bank managers and other dignitaries sat and thrashed out the pros and cons of every question and answer. If in doubt – sling it out. Good maxim. Works in all walks of life. 'When in doubt – don't.' It's now my byeword. Theoretically these meetings would cut out all problems. Practically they did – well, practically – you can never bank on what the public will do or say in any given situation. So *Gambit* gave me much laughter, but it also gave me an insight into the human mind. We've all found ourselves, at some time, thinking, 'Well, bless me soul – I've seen everything now'. Let me tell you what made *me* think that.

We had these two lovely couples on the show. Two pairs of married folk who appeared to be just there for the fun. They really didn't seem to care if they won or not: 'It's just fun to be here, Tom'. Every host has heard that a million times, and usually it's true. But what about the exceptions? Well, believe me I've seen a few, and this particular day I had the all-time classic.

In about eight minutes of card play, one team had been wiped out and their victors had accumulated an amazing haul of goodies: a TV, a refrigerator, a video, a dishwasher, a set of golf clubs, and £480 – plus the star prize, the choice of a beautiful caravan or a holiday. The holiday was a cracker: fly to New York by Concorde, spend two weeks at the Hilton Hotel and sail back on the *QE2*.

The winners decided instantly on the holiday because they

Mum and Dad at their best - together - in 1977

Mum, Dad and little Tom
in Dublin, circa 1948

Dressed in the gear, but
couldn't play cricket

Simmaries College's Rugby 2nd XV, just left of the ball
(T H Everitt & Son)

Simmaries country dance band 1960-61 - I'd handed over the
leadership to Jim Tobin *(centre)*. I'm on his left, with sticks

Were we ever that young?
(N K Howarth)

College 1958. Chess was
one of the many things
Butch Harrison taught me.
Guitar was another

Tom and Brennie - the best dressed country singers in history

Police escort and already the policemen are starting to look younger
(*courtesy of* Daily Post and Liverpool Echo)

A great array of talent, but what am I doing there?

Ma'am, please don't come to my place

A great man and a great pleasure

Home from home

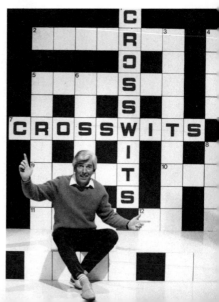

ever a cross word on *Cross Wits*
(courtesy of Tyne Tees Television)

At last America, and what exalted company

Hands up to America!

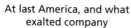

Silver wedding - twenty-five years and still going strong *(Derek Johnston*

were Jersey-based and could not take the caravan home anyway. So, choice made, fanfare of music, roll the credits, wave to the viewers and cue applause. Goodnight and God bless. And that was that – until our winning couple wrote us a letter from Jersey. They'd costed the alternative star prizes, they said, and discovered that the caravan was worth £30 more than the holiday – so would we kindly send them the balance? Did we pay? Did we hell! A free choice had been offered on screen, and they had made their choice in front of several million witnesses. There are people like that – the sort that demand change for 5p when the church collection plate comes round. Beyond the glitz and the fairylights we must always beware the 'By the Way' line. My old headmaster, Steve Brown, used to say: 'Watch the "By the Way" factor. Ignore all the preamble and waffle – wait for the line that begins, "By the way". That's the line that does the damage. That's the one which people use to cut your throat – and you don't know till you nod your head!'

Meantime, *Gambit* at Anglia ran for many series and led me to being offered *The Zodiac Game*. Another quiz show, this one was based on star signs and astrological predictions. A great idea and good for three series, despite some early reservations. It still makes me chuckle when I recall the first pilot show we made. Because of technical difficulties and first night nerves we took two hours to record a half-hour show. 'No good – it'll never work. Might as well pack it in,' moaned a Jonah from the production team. 'Why, what's the problem?' I enquired, fearing some underlying and fatal flaw in the format.

'The lady from the canteen was in the audience and she said it was too long!'

'My God,' I thought, 'one mustn't despise *vox populi*, but this is ridiculous.' How was I to change his mind? Surely not by reasoning. Certainly not by appealing to his more rational side. No, there was only one way out of this corner – attack from strength. 'Look, mush, I've done more shows than you've had hot dinners. In fact, I've done more shows than the canteen lady has *served* hot dinners. I'm not arguing with you, I'm telling you to button your lip and get on with the job!' Nasty, but it worked. The show went on – and on.

11

More of game shows and TV series later. Meantime, what was afoot on the personal front? Much in the way of comings and goings. Let's start with the family. Having extended the bounds of the Formby home as far as they could go, we decided on a major move – to a beautiful house in Southport. It was summer 1976, the year it all began for me at Thames TV, the year of the blinding hot weather, the year that Johnny Miller won the Open at Royal Birkdale. I heard him win it. 'Heard'? Yes. We'd bought 36 Waterloo Road, Birkdale. Four acres of land, swimming pool, tennis court, ten bedrooms, three storeys, double gateway, sweeping drive. And there I lay on the sun lounger by the pool listening to the golf shots over the fence and watching the Open on TV. Occasionally I glimpsed myself as the camera-laden airship flew overhead. Strange feeling, waving to yourself. Philosophical question: Should you wave back?

We were happy in Southport. Plenty of space for the family to grow. Huge hallway and massive staircase suitably decorated in stained glass – ideal for parties. Full-sized snooker table in the huge ex-dining room – ideal for entertaining TV producers and scriptwriters. Our house was part of 'celebrity row' and it was a little unnerving when the local holiday camp tour bus passed by us and we could hear the tour guide intoning:

'On your left is Kenny Dalglish. Over there Tom O'Connor. A little further along is Billy Bingham.'

It gave the impression of a bus load of burglars making notes on gates, alarms and security devices. No problems though: touch wood, not one attempted burglary. Instead, a chance to relax a little and soak up the amazing number of events that had happened to our little family in so short a time. A momentous phone call asked if I would appear on the Royal Variety Show before the Queen Mother. Nearly stopped my heart entirely, that show. Nobody's fault really, but what a scary do. My old pal Roger de Courcey and I shared a pretty stark room at the London Palladium. Still we'd brought in some lager and we had plenty of laughs. A huge cast of entertainers expertly chosen by Lord Delfont and hosted by Max Bygraves were lined up to fill three hours of live and two hours of recorded variety material. My own slot followed some time after Roger's, but I was not too nervous to watch and admire his performance. I'll never forget Nookie's lines about the Queen's silver jubilee.

'We're having a street party twenty-two miles long.'

'Where's that going to be?' asked Roger.

'Well, you know that lane of the M1 motorway that's coned off? ...'

Seventeen years later that gag still works – the lane is still regularly blocked off. Whatever will happen to Britain when all the roadworks are complete – we'll have another three million unemployed, and the Isle of Wight will be a dumping ground for cones and flashing beacons!

Back, though, to the show and my major problem. A certain top French entertainer, who shall be nameless, declared his refusal to bow to the royal box.

'You would not bow to our queen,' he argued.

'But you cut her head off!' replied a bright spark, smiling grimly.

'They can't order you to do anything, you know,' said Max Bygraves. 'They can only ask you. They want you to close part one in an open ended spot.'

I'd prepared a routine of six minutes including a song. But now, if the moody Frenchman refused to go on, I could end up doing twenty-five! How would I know how long to do? Simple – the bandleader would stand up when I had two minutes to go. Muggins, I nodded my head, went on and sweated blood. Laughs? I got a few. Applause? A modicum. Minutes? Only six. Oh yes, Frenchie went on; oh yes, the bandleader stood up with two minutes to go. He needn't have bothered. I've watched the TV replay a dozen times since. I never took my eyes off him – I performed the entire show to the pit: never looked up, never moved my gaze from his white dinner jacket and white hair. The audience only saw the top of my head – not enough to form an opinion. The Royal Variety Show was a let down for me.

Not so *This is Your Life*. Oh boy, did that surprise me. It came about so quickly I could hardly take it in. I was filming a comedy show at the studios in Teddington and had hardly any time to breathe. Not a lover of autocue or prompt cards, I insisted on learning every word of the script and re-working every sketch until it was second nature. This needs an iron will. I didn't have it but William G Stewart, my producer, did. It was a great show, but certain off-stage things just were not right. All day, no word from Pat or from mum, dad or the kids. Very strange. 'Don't bother ringing home, boss,' said Tommy, my roadie. 'I've already checked it out. Everything's OK.'

'Blow you, mate,' I thought, 'I'm the one to check if all's well.' So I rang home. No answer. Odd. Rang my parents' home. Nothing. Peculiar.

What I didn't know, of course, was that the O'Connor tribe were gathering in London for a briefing and rehearsal with Eamon Andrews. They would pounce on me at the weakest moment, just as the TV show ended and I was about to relax. What they didn't know was the trauma I was undergoing, worrying about my family. Roadie Tommy was sacked three times that day. Who the hell kept reinstating him I do not know!

I remember Lionel Blair saying to me once: 'If Eamon catches you, try to remember the first thing that crosses your mind.' On his 'Life', Lionel had been approached in the street and wondered why on earth Eamon was wearing make up!

I was caught as I took a final bow in the studio. I turned and saw the man and thought: 'It's Eamon Andrews' smaller brother.' Then I saw the red book. Because he always appeared in the foreground on the show I'd assumed Eamon was about 6 ft 4 in; in fact he was about 5 ft 10 in. But it was him all right and, boy, was I caught! It's a little known fact that after he has agreed to be 'done', there's a break for the victim whilst the cameras are reset, chairs and props arranged and audiences settled down. During this period I quaffed a large brandy and prayed out loud to the researchers that they wouldn't produce a face from the past that I couldn't recognise. They didn't. I knew them all, friends, family, pupils, work mates, club owners – oh, and the legendary Charlie Wilson. Charlie was the concert secretary of a club in Toxteth, Peel Hall. He'd booked me many times, always paying top dollar and ever ready to fill a date if I needed work. He'd even come prepared on my big night. As he recited his piece to camera, he leaned across and whispered in my ear: 'There's a half bottle in me inside pocket if you need a swig.' Thanks, Charlie, only you would think of that.

It was a great night, tempered by the thought of a long day's recording tomorrow. Above all, perhaps, the video has given me a permanent record of people I loved and subsequently lost. My mother, Uncle Tom, Steve Brown, club owner John Allinson. They'd even found Father Frank

Carey, a white missionary from Zambia, who was bundled onto a plane in his tropical clothes and shuffled into Heathrow in mid-winter. He's back in Africa now – and he took my bicycle with him. Hey, Frank – that was only a loan, you know!

The media bandwagon continued to roll on and every facet of my life and that of the family was covered by radio, TV, newspapers and magazines. It seemed that almost daily we were being photographed and interviewed for this or that feature, and we all became expert in the posing business. Basically you take up a stance, and set a particular facial expression, and if it hurts you've got it right! Pictures with golf clubs, pictures on swings, pictures with animals – they were all taken. Did I say pictures with animals? Next to page 3 models they are the most difficult and possibly the most dangerous.

To be fair to the fairer sex and to the more beautifully endowed members, I've only had a limited number of experiences of working with the glamour side of photography. The first was when a daily tabloid requested a picture of me being kissed on the cheek by a (fully clad) model. The major mistake I made was to agree to the shots being taken at my house. This entailed a two-hour recce by the photographer, disturbing every room and dissecting every item of my wardrobe before setting up the job. It also entailed the late arrival of Miss X – busty, leggy, yet possibly not the full shilling. To say she took forever to get ready is an understatement – after an hour and three-quarters I gave the reporter an ultimatum – either we did the shots straight away, or I'd need to go and have another shave and haircut! Once bitten, I learned never to allow long, uncontrollable photo sessions at home. Use a studio where the limits of time, and his expense account, prevail.

Different events made for different memories and more often than not those memories were of fun and enjoyment. Take the case of *Organ Monthly*. You what? Yes, *Organ*

Monthly, a very fine publication, but one which at first sight
has little to do with what my act is about. In my time I'd
had excellent reason to appreciate the skills of organists and
the wonderful machines they play. On many an occasion
the ability of the musician to busk along with my tuneless
warblings had saved my fee, if not my life, in clubs. And
while every club comic has a story damning the organist
for one thing or another, I have only praise and gratitude
to heap on him or her. Wasn't it a lady who, by accident,
picked up the wrong envelope one night and took my £20
whilst I went home without checking my fee and was left
with £4. Wasn't it that same lady, who rang my school
the next morning to agree a time to call and give me the
balance?

Then there was Tommy, an incredible man who played
a mighty Wurlitzer in a Wigan club and made even the
squawkiest singer sound like Sinatra? Who but the enlight-
ened few knew that Tommy was blind, made his own braille
notes on what keys and what tempos each singer required.
Tommy's guide dog was a beautiful Labrador called Peggy.
She'd lie at Tommy's feet by the organ pedals and gently
snooze through all the noise and crescendos of a Saturday
night. She only moved when somebody sang a bum note –
then she'd growl fiercely and glare at the culprit. I had many
a growl and glare from Peggy over the years. I'd like to
think she made me a better singer. I'd like to, but I can't.

So back to the accolade by *Organ Monthly*, for accolade
it certainly was. The request was for a picture of me at the
business end of a new electronic organ, looking busy. Me?
A man of no ability at the keyboard? Yes. Apparently many
non-players had featured in this type of shot, including that
great snooker champion Ray Reardon. OK – if it was good
enough for one of my heroes, it was certainly good enough
for me. Anyway, it would help on two fronts. The obvious
one was publicity, then the second was the chance to
decorate our newly acquired house down south. Another

house? Well, a kind of London-ish retreat really. A two-bedroomed detached, split-level affair in Sandhurst. It would be ideal as a base while I was filming at Thames TV, and it was a surefire investment in the days when all smart-thinking investment gurus urged: 'Buy land, they've stopped making it!'

Our little southern hideaway was up a hill in a beautiful corner called Cock-a-Dobby, and was the ideal, quiet setting amidst friendly, gentle neighbours. Friendly that is until the *Organ Monthly* day. It seemed that the feature demanded genuine atmosphere. Not for us the faked background of a studio or a music store sales room. No, it had to be a picture taken in my own abode and showing the trappings of whatever room could hold the organ. Hold the organ? Yes, indeed. Because for us there would not be a small or even medium-sized keyboard: we were getting the whole shebang and then some! The full Wurlitzing works! So one early spring morning down leafy and dormant Cock-a-Dobby came this vast pantechnicon, grinding gears and exhaling diesel smoke. The arrival stirred me into action and I sprang to the door with only one thought in mind – how the blue blazes was the vehicle going to get back out again? Certainly it would not have enough room to turn round, and lord knows how it could be reversed back. Still if that was troubling my mind, much more was troubling the neighbours.

They watched as, slowly big bit by little bit, organ pipe by organ pipe, the monster was carried into our house. Minute by minute indeed hour by hour, the van rose higher off the ground as the weight decreased, and the house seemed to settle by inches as the weight was transferred. At last the deed was done and the fitters began to connect the various wires and clips to assemble the instrument. Then they gave it a cursory but none too quiet test for volume. I swear that one burst of discord dislodged several tiles.

Our neighbours separately, but simultaneously, remarked:

'Hell's teeth! What sort of man is this who fills his entire lounge with the trappings of Cape Canaveral? Maybe he's a religious freak who's going to blast out hymns at ungodly hours. Maybe, worse still, he's a mad sadist who's bent on playing "Chopsticks" for all eternity at a million decibels.'

I tried to explain the real reason for the presence of the organ. Unfortunately, when the magazine came out it made me look somewhat of a liar. The organ was there all right, so too was I looking almost capable of playing it, but there was no background – the organ filled the entire page. I could have been sat in a field, or a studio, or even a music shop! Still, the feature was done, the organ was seen to be disassembled and reloaded into the truck. How the truck got down the hill backwards I'll never know: I went off to the local with the few neighbours still speaking to me and waited till the coast was clear!

So, houses north and south, pictures here, there and everywhere, non-stop TV and cabaret work. How was this affecting the standing of the family generally? Well, the good thing was that it affected the children not a jot. They'd grown up coping with the increasing popularity of their dad – luckily there was no overnight success. Similarly, our friends remained our friends and do to this day. Gradually, we all learned to live with fame and never let the glitter and fairylights dictate our outlook or actions. To a certain extent I feel sorry for pools jackpot winners and others who suddenly find fame and have no chance to adapt to the pressures.

Much safer is the way that I trod, from humble beginnings, through hard times and harder times to the edges of the big time, always listening, always trying to learn from those who knew and those who'd made it. Always, too, taking note of the reaction of those in my particular trade – the comics, the funny men, the last of the heroes, the men who had no back up but their shadows on the floor. How would these latter day gunfighters feel about one of their ilk making it in a slightly different sphere? Would there be envy? Would there be malice?

Here I'm certain was another case of my getting lucky. If the good lord had offered a free choice of fellow travellers on the road to the jokers' paradise I could not have picked better companions. All of them grafters, none of them whingers, their common response was delight because one of their number had 'cracked it'. Like musketeers of old it was one for all and all for the main chance. Let's hope we all make it 'down the road'.

The great gods of TV determined that I was ready for the nod – ripe for choice as a front man who would succeed and, more importantly, survive the cauldron. But it must have been a close call with some of my contemporaries. When you hear my case for their selection I think you'll agree that the gods were kind and possibly blind in giving me preference.

Take Jackie Hamilton, one of the best comedians Liverpool has ever produced. He's a naturally funny man, with a sharp brain, outrageous line in quips and a beautiful visual manner. Like the great Tommy Cooper, Jackie can produce tears of laughter without saying a word. People stream home from his shows marvelling at his brilliance but unable to explain exactly *what* he did – surely the mark of true genius. Other than the odd shot on *The Comedians*, history can produce no film clips of this great man, although it was so nearly a different story. A straight acting part and the chance of endless TV repeats would have been within his grasp but for his healthy looks. He must weigh around 200 lb, possibly more, and this was his undoing in the legendary confrontation with the big time.

TV were making a series called *Tenko*, the tale of women captured by the Japanese in World War 2, and they were in search of different locations. Southport was chosen for the last two episodes. In order to fill in the bit parts and walk-ons it was decided to recruit union members from the local area. This would save a fortune in overnight expenses and rail fares. And so it was that Jackie Hamilton's name was put forward as a Japanese prisoner of war. On the fateful day our hero stood behind the wire clad only in knee length khaki shorts, his heroic paunch gleaming stark white in the sunshine, straining against an old snake-buckle belt from Boy Scout days. Along the set stepped the film director, coat off shoulders in true Hollywood style, gazing searchingly at the assembled throng behind the wire. 'You!' he suddenly bellowed at Jackie. 'You – the very white chap! Get away. You can't be a Japanese prisoner of war that shape!!'

'But I was only captured yesterday,' retorted Hamilton. Collapse of brutal camp guards, prisoners, film crew, TV executives and anyone else within earshot.

And then again, what of Eddie Flanagan, surely the wackiest and most lovable of all the Merseyside fun pack. God rest you, Eddie my friend – there'll never be another like you.

'It's gear here, isn't it?' Not the most blistering opening line, but it served to centre attention on a big, genial face that sparkled with mischief and fun.

'Two blokes hunting bears in Canada. They were driving along and saw a sign saying "Bear Left". So they went home!'

No, not the world's most satirical patter, more like a primary school joke. But words on the page can never convey timing or vocal inflexion or any of the other resources deployed by Eddie. He could make laughter in a graveyard. He could make the most obscure situation hysterical. In his local pub one of the regular customers was a detective inspector. Eddie never drew attention to this, but every time the policeman came in, Eddie would wrap a hanky around his glass while drinking. Did the cop see the fingerprint joke? Or was it just there to be laughed at by ghosts or angels? Or consider the case of the garden gnomes. Eddie's next door neighbour was potty about gnomes – he bought them by the truck load and they festooned all parts of his little back garden: gnomes on swings, gnomes on toadstools – probably gnomes on the loo if you looked closely enough. All this passion for little plaster men began to get to Eddie. Every time he looked into his neighbour's garden he felt affronted. Eventually he decided that the only thing to be done was to organise a kidnapping raid and to spirit away the pointy-hatted ones.

The timing of the deed was crucial: there must be no witnesses and there must be watertight alibis. Eddie must be proven to have been elsewhere at the vital hour. Why not Spain? That was far enough away to satisfy even the detective inspector from the pub. So tickets were booked and a hotel reserved. Mr and Mrs Flanagan rose extra early that summer's morn and, pausing only to snatch the prime gnome from over the fence, set off in their overladen car to the south coast and the ferry. Nothing was heard for three days. And then, the breakthrough in police enquiries. From somewhere on the Costa del Sol came a postcard written by 'Nicky the Gnome'. It read: 'Having a great time. Don't try to look for me.' This was the first of several such cards over the next fortnight. And then nothing. No word from the plaster person until Eddie's return – and then what a shock for his fretting neighbour. Nicky the gnome had been put back in his old place in the garden and, after fourteen days in Spain, his hands and face had acquired a lovely dark tan. See you 'down the road', Eddie!

Wherefore are they now, those fellow comics of mine from the early days? Some are gone, some go on forever. Stevie Faye was the most original and anarchic of all. A constant companion on shows when I was just a singer, Stevie seemed to have the ability and the material to do a different show every night:

'Coal-delivery man stops his horse and cart and orders his lad: "Take a sack up to the flat on the 14th floor." Off staggers the lad, up 14 floors, and returns still clutching the sack.'

'What's wrong, lad?'

'She wants two!'

'OK, take a big sack.'

Grunts and groans from the lad: 'It's no good boss, I can't budge it. I can't!'

'Relax, boy – you've got the horse by the ears!'

Ah, Stevie. The funny man, the constant worker for charity, the unfailing source of advice when I was but a showbiz sprog. Let me recall one of those tales that are typical of you. Will you settle for the policeman's helmet?

The two constant scourges of an entertainer are the clock and the speeding laws. He always seems to be behind hand. He can wake up an hour earlier than necessary – and in a few minutes find he is way behind schedule. All that can be done is to speed things up and hope there are no traffic jams, no careless day-dreaming drivers, no drunks if the journey is after closing time. Having just come off stage, his brain is hyper-active. He would not be able to relax or sleep for a few hours yet, so he might as well get in the car and go at least part of the way to the next venue. What happens if long distances have to be covered at awkward times, what if the act must go whilst the roads are cluttered? It's then that the speed limits tend to get ignored: forty becomes fifty-five; seventy climbs to eighty. Eyes must be peeled for chasing oncoming patrol cars and radar traps.

Steve tried to neutralise this problem by the wonderfully simple expedient of placing a policeman's helmet in the back window of his Ford Granada. He was convinced that any traffic cop would take pity on a brother officer and spare him the speeding tickets. For years it seemed to work – or maybe he was just lucky to avoid patrols. But he got his come-uppance in the north-east of England, where a patrol car flagged him down. The officer appeared at his window:

'I see you're in the force.'

'Yes, mate.'

'Which town?'

'Liverpool.'

'Oh, yeah. What division?'

'The first!' muttered football-mad Faye, just before he was nicked.

Stevie, Stevie, what would the general think of you? The general? You know, Mike Hughes. Mike was an agent in the early Liverpool club days. He booked only comics and had a huge circuit. He sent Steve to a club near Rhyl, where Steve bombed out, and then got into an altercation with the committee. So serious was the row that the club rang Mike Hughes to complain.

'I've started to call Mike Hughes the General,' Steve said to me later.

'Why?'

'He's just rung me up and said: "You've cost me Wales!"'

Mike lost Wales — but he gained Russ Abbot, whom he manages today and with whom he's forged one of the most successful act/management bonds in entertainment.

12

'You've got to be a comedian to live in Liverpool.' This ancient tag is not a million miles from the truth. To test the water as a would-be comic, I would suggest you listen to the everyday humour of the Scouser. Bus conductors, for instance:

'Do you stop at the Adelphi Hotel?'

'What, on my wages?'

Or, bus passengers:

'Do you go to the Pier Head?'

'Yeah, inside only.'

'Well, where does upstairs go then?'

Or taxi drivers. In 1989, on the ride from my hotel to the Empire Theatre, I remarked:

'I may be wrong, but I'm beginning to feel the old buzz back in the town.'

'Nah, mate. This place is still on the floor,' the driver snapped over his shoulder.

'Are you sure? I mean the eyes seem brighter, the shoulders higher.'

'Nah! You're wrong, lad. This town is still on the deck. I'll tell you how bad things are – it's eight months since somebody's been sick in the back of this car!' That's certainly damning evidence in anyone's book, isn't it? But all's not gloom and doom on the taxi front. Take two stories that came to my ears. The first involved that holy of holies, Yates's wine lodge. There are several of these emporiums scattered world-wide, and they are basically bars which specialise in the sale of Australian white wine, mostly plonk. Many and varied are the jokes and anecdotes surrounding the wine lodge, from petrol bombs being drunk to new types of wine, for instance the 'Back-to-school drink – two glasses and you're in a class of your own!'

The regular drinkers have been involved in many an escapade. One cabbie was called to the lodge in Moorfields, Liverpool, to pick up a fare. With some trepidation he pulled up outside. There stood, or rather swayed, his charge. On seeing the cab, he staggered over and slumped down in the back, mumbling:

'Yates' wine lodge, pal.' He then began to snore.

The cabbie pondered the problem for a few minutes. Then he released the brakes, allowed the cab to roll forward a few yards, and pulled up.

'We're there, mate,' he called out to his fare.

'Wha?'

'We're there. Yates'.'

Groans and angry mumbling from the back. Then:

'How much?'

'Call it three quid for cash.'

'Here you are, then. And next time, not so fast!'

Tales of taxis inevitably rekindle memories of Eric Merriman. Eric is a very fine scriptwriter, particularly brilliant in the field of comic songs and parodies. In their time people like Russ Abbot and Marti Caine have been grateful for his efforts. Eric and I were working on a show together and we were reminiscing about our home town of Liverpool, and one thing led to another. 'Taxi drivers?' said Eric. 'Well, what about my brother?'

It seems the other Merriman was a black-cab driver and had been on holiday for a fortnight. On returning to the depot he was told that his particular vehicle was off the road for servicing.

'Go to the workshop and take number 119,' the manager said.

Eric's brother duly did as he was told and, without double-checking all features and trusting in the efficiency of the mechanics, he set off cruising for trade. After a while he got a radio call to pick up a Chinese seaman on the dock road.

Sure enough the bloke was at the right spot, and the cabbie pulled alongside and said, 'Hop in, mate. Where are you going?'

Mumbling the name of a restaurant in Chinatown, the sailor disappeared into the back and off sped the taxi. At the first set of lights the driver pulled up at red, glanced in his mirror and realised that the Chinaman was missing!

'My God, he's fallen out,' thought Merriman. 'Now I'm for it – first day back as well!' Creeping anxiously to the rear of the cab, he found a sight to behold. The cab, it later emerged, had been in the workshop for major repairs to the rear end, and, in order to achieve access to it, the back seat had been removed, and had not been replaced. The Chinaman was sitting on the floor, seemingly quite content.

When I hear stories like that, I never question them, for I've learned that there is nothing funnier than the truth. Jokes are merely an extension of reality, made more acceptable by the fact that they are about somebody else. As a consequence, all my favourite comics tend to be tellers of the true or nearly true tale. I love enlargers of life, observers of humanity, people who can find wit in the humdrum and humour even in sadness. There are the people whose style and eloquence will never die, but merely be passed on to younger, eager takers. Sonny Day was a funny little man whose gentle presentation allowed his punchlines to steal up on you.

'I've got this new girlfriend. I met her at a dance. I said: "Are you with anybody?"

'She said, "Yes, I'm with anybody!"'

Or take the more direct approach of Jack Platts: 'The wife keeps saying I never take her anywhere, so I gave her a dig in the ribs at 6.30 this morning and said: "Are you coming down the pit?"'

Or Joe Kenyon, dry as a bone: 'If Widnes lose one more match they'll fall out of the paper.'

Joe it is who still holds the record for the bravest-ever opening quip. Appearing in Jarrow, home of the brave and redoubtable hunger marchers, he strode to the mike one Sunday lunchtime and said:

'Good afternoon, Jarrow, how's your feet?' They let him live – in fact, they laughed.

Such were some of the people with whom I'd grown up and honed my skills. These were the heroes I would remember as my career took a ninety degree turn away from social clubs and the fast-fading nightclubs. These were the days I would remember when the going got tough in the TV world and all that was there to stiffen my sinews was experience and the thought that 'the lads wouldn't let this beat them, so neither will I.'

Easy to write of these things now, in the knowledge that all went well, but in the heat of change and the security of new and more demanding roles there is always scepticism and fear. The fear of failure, the fear of self-destruction – it's amazing how heavily they weigh in the mind of the funnyman when decisions have to be taken.

For many reasons, not worth the listing, I found it necessary to leave *Name that Tune* and cast around for other challenges. I shall never be more sad than I was when I left that show. It felt like losing a loved one, a family bereavement. Still, it had to be done and all that can be done in a case like that is to wipe the eyes and not look back.

I came over to the BBC. They offered me many things, and they delivered. They gave me more outlets to test my skill, my endurance, and my patience. To begin with I had to learn the BBC way of doing things – slow but steady. Never would I dare to suggest: 'At Thames we did it this way' – that was the cue for a severe ear bashing.

Instead, I studied, I toiled and I learned. We produced three comedy series – not brilliant, not mind-blowing in their intensity, but reasonably funny and harmless in their targets. But the Lord is wondrous in his workings and one move in life's plan can trigger another, one meeting can ignite the fuse under a fresh idea. So it was, in 1983, that I became involved with one of my favourite Welshmen, Phil Lewis. Head of BBC2 Outside Broadcasts, Phil had two bees in his bonnet: good clean humour, and 'real people' television. How he must smile, in his retirement, at the extent to which the better-rated shows of today reflect his ideas and his passions.

When I was first approached by this witty gent and he explained his plan for me, I sat back and remembered the old Lancashire adage: 'When you're out of your depth, keep your gob shut and your ears open.'

This I did with a vengeance and allowed my ballooning eyes to display my eagerness to host Phil's pet project: *I've Got a Secret*. Basically it was to be a show that would combine the best of *This Is Your Life* and *What's My Line*. We would feature ordinary folk who had done extraordinary things – war heroes, pioneers in various fields, people lucky to survive disasters, folks who achieved the funniest, the most remarkable, the best and the worst. All human life and all human oddities were there, and what a gift that was for the fast-developing O'Connor – still searching for the Holy Grail of the successful TV show.

What set out as a TV parlour game gradually developed into a top-rated show, rewarded with a Friday evening slot and four consecutive series. We featured life at its funniest, its bravest, its most quirky. From the heroics of the first man ashore on D-Day to a lady who was bitten by a crocodile in a flat in Wolverhampton and to a man who exported plaster palm trees to Arabs – the celebrity panel were forever kept on their toes. Good clean family fare and plenty of scope for me to ad lib and genuinely relax before the cameras.

If you are enjoying doing a project and it seems to be going well, there's always the chance that you'll get carried away by enthusiasm and the sheer momentum of events. And this often results in one taking what, in hindsight, were absurd decisions. It's even more difficult to be healthily sceptical about one's judgement when you are surrounded by people extolling your talent. Through hard work, study, experience and luck, I had a cast-iron show, and I began to believe, if only a little, in my own invincibility. But I was in for a shock. And yet it started off, as so many disasters do, on the back of good intentions.

In retrospect it probably wasn't a good idea to put an Englishman in charge of a New Year's Eve show live from Scotland. As it was, a whole battalion of Caledonian gremlins did their worst. Gleneagles was the prestigious setting for the event and I arrived a day early just to recce the scene. I soon realised that all was not tickety-boo, as they say. For a show that would be about 90 minutes 'live', there was very little stand-by material on tape. So if there was a 'cock-up' there would be nothing to run on film while we covered our tracks. Eventually we decided to record one of the bands. This saved our lives literally. Because of sound problems (the speakers were tiny and placed under tables – not the best place in a room full of merrymakers) and other major setbacks, the rehearsals became merely a walk through and in general a potentially disastrous hit-and-hope mentality prevailed.

Fortunately, in Moira Anderson, Chic Murray and Maggie Moone I had experienced campaigners who would not let me down when the crunch came. It began well with the party indoors bouncing with health and enthusiasm and tucking into the finest foods and beverages. The opening piece to camera was fine. So was the opening music by the pipe band, who were freezing outside in the car park but, thank God, miming to a pre-recorded tape. Moira sang, the country danceband played, I cracked the odd gag and then the bottom fell out of the proceedings.

The pipe band came in and marched up and down the dance floor. Then they should have marched out, but they stayed where they were, completely blocking Chic Murray's mark. Poor old Chic should have come on with a glass of Scotch and a lump of coal to bring in the New Year. Not being able to find his mark, he had no camera to talk to, so he gagged as best he could to the audience – who could hardly hear him because of the sound problems.

The director decided to cut to our guest actor, who was to recite a humorous Scottish poem. This began well – then tapered off as the man forgot the words. Back cut the cameras, this time to yours truly, without the aid of an earpiece.

'Talk to Camera 3 and be funny – now!!' said the floor manager. How long for? What would I say?

'I've just come from the bar and . . .' I heard myself saying, while desperately scrambling for a stunning gag. None came.

Back we cut to lovely Maggie Moone sporting a slinky dress and attempting to vamp a table full of half-cut guys in kilts.

'I'll kill him,' cried Maggie's husband as one gallant laddie put his hand up her skirt. Maggie (and believe me, I've watched the replay) remained unflinching and pounded out the song until the order came to cut back to T O'C.

'Talk to Camera 3, be funny – now!!' came the order. Talk about *déjà-vu*.

'There's a bloke in the bar who . . .' But again the search for a life-saver proved fruitless.

By now the boisterous audience was treating the thing as one huge wind-up. So they decided to turn the whole proceedings into a party.

'You won't believe what I've just seen in the bar...' were the last words I said on that show. A millisecond later the plug was pulled and we left the network never to return. What a catastrophe! I've still got the video – it's labelled on the spine: 'The Show that Died of Shame'. Hours later Pat and I and Maggie and Colin, her husband, sat and speculated miserably on the possible outcome.

'It's not so bad for me,' said Maggie, 'I'm not that well known, but you – you've had it.' I was inclined to agree.

'Who knows,' said Colin. 'Maybe no one was watching, or maybe they were too drunk to notice.' Not true, alas. One person who was watching that night was Michael Grade, boss of BBC Light Entertainment at the time. For some reason he saw my performance in a good light – perhaps he appreciated the desperation that made me fight to the last pub joke to save the sinking ship. Whatever the reason, I found just enough favour to be considered for the role that above all others I have loved performing: host of a live TV variety show.

The Tom O'Connor Road Show was the brainchild of the good folk at Pebble Mill, and was a vehicle for all the best in variety. Guest stars and up-and-coming pop groups, members of the public displaying their talent for singing, spoon-playing, dancing or whatever – a live game show with plenty of interesting scenery and local colour. We visited a different town or city each week. We would set up camp in civic halls or theatres and went out live on the network from 12.30 pm to 1 pm Monday to Friday. The half-hour final product was the result of very hard work by a huge team of people. Researchers, writers, directors, producers, lights, sound, cameras, make-up – you name them, we had them. It was like a huge circus moving around Britain – attracting not a little attention as we went.

Many lessons had been learned since the early days of our pilot show in Telford, where the local radio gave out the details of the venue and asked literally anyone to come along and appear on TV. We had bus loads of wannabees – people who caught bullets in their teeth, soot-jugglers, people who could nail jelly to the ceiling – all human oddities were there. By the time of transmission, however, we'd tempered the rush by liaising up front with the local media and researching into people's backgrounds. We still had wondrous sights on stage, like the tap dancer, Condor. As I recall he was an architect who loved to spend his time clad as a bird and living in a linen basket. Despite all our efforts though, the good British public were not to be put off easily. It became quite the thing for people to find out which hotel we were using and come along to audition. Due to the need for topical gags it became imperative for me to retire early, about 9 pm, and rise about 5 am to check all news items for angles. This meant that I never drank and hardly had any chance for relaxation except for the odd knock of golf. It also meant that I would be off the hotel scene before would-be entertainers got drunk enough to approach the team with their efforts. I was able to witness a few, though, and I suppose my favourite had to be the man in Falkirk. The writers and myself were enjoying a coffee in the corner of the lounge when in walked a tall gentleman dressed completely as a Christmas tree. Together with roots, leaves, and star on the top, he was probably eight feet high, and as we stared in wonder he lit up – head to foot he glowed in fairy lights.

'By gum, that's impressive isn't it?' I asked one of our electricians.

'Yes, but the berk's plugged himself straight into the mains: he's a walking suicide.'

So, sadly, the audition failed and a star was dismissed from the firmament. Still, there would be plenty more. People who juggled burning sticks, a lady who made ladders out of paper, poetry readers, comedians and others who, albeit unconsciously, stole the show. It was while we were at Portsmouth that I heard one of the best put-downs. He was a young royal marine, aged about 21, and he was taking us on the guided tour of HMS *Victory*. Our party included a group of French tourists.

'Excuse me,' enquired one of them. 'Zees cannonballs.' 'Zees are what you used at Trafalgar?'

'Oh no,' replied the marine, 'your navy's still got them!'

What an answer. Makes you feel proud. Hell, it makes you feel jealous that you didn't get the chance to say it! So much for worrying about the young folk. To those who doubt the talents, ingenuity and staying power of today's children I say "socks" – they are as sharp and intelligent as ever we were – more in fact. If anyone has doubts about the quality of today's children, my best advice is to try entertaining them. Especially pantomime, when you have to attempt to make 3000 kids believe what you're saying and doing. I thought I knew it all – thirteen years a teacher, and a father of four – but believe me they are no training ground for dealing with children who have paid to be entertained.

Often I'm asked for quotes from my teaching days. One of my favourites was the five-year-old who was busily drawing a picture in crayon.

'What's that you're doing?' enquired the teacher.

'I'm drawing God,' came the reply.

'But no one knows what God looks like.'

'They will when I've finished.'

In panto, it soon became painfully apparent to me that if I were to appear on stage, 6 ft tall and grey haired, and pretend to be a mischievous teenager called 'Buttons', some serious work would have to be done on the patter.

'Hi, kids, my name's Buttons and I'm in love with Cinderella' was my first-ever line in panto. 'I'm going to marry her, you know.'

'No, you're not, I've read the book' came a shout from a front-row four-year-old.

Back to the drawing board, O'Connor!

When your luck's in, though, your luck's in, and once again the Almighty gave me light in the darkness. My early panto life was shaped by the wonderful partnership of Tommy Trafford and Ronnie Parnell. Tommy, my first 'mother', was the best dame I ever appeared with – no teeth, but plenty of talent. Spectacular costumes, windmills, traffic lights, Christmas trees. Best timer of a visual gag I ever met, he would try anything new just for a laugh. When a gag failed, he would deliver the unforgettable line, 'High Park were never like this!' It meant absolutely nothing but would reduce both of us to hysterics – a state which swiftly encompassed the whole audience.

'There's nothing funnier than a whole room full of people laughing at nowt!' was Tommy's maxim. His partner and erstwhile producer, Ronnie, was the last of the song-and-dance men. Great presence on stage, master of the long stare, particularly at an uppity young comic trying to ad lib. Ronnie's wife, Marie Ashton, was our choreographer and generally appeared as a character called Mabel, a servant girl. It was only after she'd pointed it out herself that I realised that invariably her part would be that of a fetcher and carrier.

'Where's the baron? Mabel go and find him.'

'Cinderella! Cinderella! Mabel, go and look in the stables for her.'

'Mabel, tell the sisters that the prince is here.'

After the show, in the pub across the road, Marie would say:

'I'm just popping out. If Ronnie asks, tell him I've gone to look for someone!'

These lovely people collectively secured my position as a panto comic by their kindness, advice and perseverance. They helped open my eyes to the wonder of the live stage play, the opportunity it offers to touch the minds and emotions of the very young and the very old, to help transport the thoughts and dreams of a room full of people to the ends of the rainbow.

All this was spelled out to me as I worked hard at the trade of pantomime, learning the rules and gathering in a treasury of funny tales. There seems to be no other branch of the industry that attracts as many anecdotes – true or not, who cares?

From the very early days of popular singers becoming panto stars and having to find a reason to perform, we have the cave scene in *Aladdin* when our hero rubs the magic lamp. Out pops the genie and roars:

'Your wish is my command, O Master. Speak and I obey.'

'I wish to hear Issy Bonn singing "Goldmine in the sky",' orders Aladdin.

'It shall be done, O Master.' And on comes dear old Issy in cabaret attire – in the middle of the deserts of Arabia.

Then there was the tale of the cheapest-ever production of *Aladdin* ever produced: Shoestring Promotions Limited.

Scene: The Cave. A knocking from outside.

'Who is without?' enquires Aladdin.

''Tis Ali Baba and the forty thieves.'

'Come in Ali Baba, and bring *two* of the thieves with you!!'

Worse still was Snow White with a shortage in the dwarf department. Finances had prevented the hiring of the customary seven small folk, so only two were used and they would march across the back of the set with a pole with five heads attached and screened behind a hedge.

Then there was Snow White in Belfast – more dwarf problems. This time not too few but too many. Eleven, to be exact. What to do? Leave it to the producer, a very stern lady indeed.

'Now look,' she said, 'we've too many dwarfs. Four of you will have to go!'

'But we've come from all over Europe,' chirped a little fellow.

'I don't care where you've come from. The title is *Snow White and the Seven Dwarfs*. Four of you will have to go. I'm going to audition each of you. As I call out your name, run across and do a cartwheel. OK?'

'But I can't do cartwheels,' moaned one of the senior members.

'Now tell me,' said the stern lady, 'what is the bloody point of being a dwarf if you can't do cartwheels?' Good question. But if you are a dwarf like my mate Kenny Baker, funny man, brilliant musician, film actor, there's no end to the tricks you can pull. Kenny, along with 64 others, was auditioning at the Prince of Wales Theatre, London.

'Look, Ken,' said the producer, 'most of these guys can be dismissed straight off – those who can't sing, and those who can't speak perfect English.'

'I know,' replied Kenny, 'but they won't leave. They want to wait here till the end of the auditions. Then we'll all leave together.'

'But why wait?' queried the bossman.

'Because we want to see the looks on the faces of the bus drivers when they see 65 dwarfs crossing Piccadilly Circus at the same time!' laughed Kenny.

I've had my share of near disasters at panto time, I can tell you. I'll be content here to tell you about a couple of them. One involved old Harry, who was in his mid-eighties and was a life-long friend of Tommy Trafford, Ronnie Parnell and his wife Marie. In his younger days Harry had been many things – singer, female impersonator, dog trainer. Now he lived only for showbusiness, and in 1975 he was the pit pianist for us at Southport. The main problem was that Harry was inclined to fall asleep at any time – even in mid-tune!

Obviously, this slowed things down a bit and made one wish to emit a piercing, hysterical scream, so a 'real' organist was also employed to drown both Harry's many discordant notes and his frequent snoring. In one production of *Cinderella*, Tommy and I found ourselves reciting the lines whilst staring at Harry's still frame slumped over the keyboard.

'Dead,' mouthed Tommy. 'Dead for sure.'

'Never happened when I was on,' I mouthed back.

'Died while Ronnie was singing, I'll bet,' Tommy retorted.

'Keep going and leave him there till the interval,' prompted Ronnie from off-stage.

So the show rumbled on, entrances, exits, with Mabel (Marie) searching for people as usual, and Harry's head resting on the ivories. They the moment came for Cinderella to be transformed into a beautiful princess and me (Buttons) to stand weeping and waving as her coach rolled off. At precisely this emotional second, Harry awoke from the dead and began playing where he'd left off!! So the coach exited, and I shed noisy tears, to the thumping strains of the overture, 'On a wonderful day like today'. I don't know what the audience thought. I know what I thought, however: 'I'm going to skin Harry alive.' Even worse was to happen to Simple Simon – and guess who was playing *him*.

This time it was *Jack and the Beanstalk* and again it caused Ronnie Parnell a lot of grief. We'd had a couple of minor glitches in the production already. Tommy Trafford's entrance was on a swing, which was suspended about 30 feet above the stage; there he perched for the opening ten minutes of the show, before his cue. All went well until one day we noticed that the great man had fallen asleep and was being kept aloft by balance alone. You won't believe the lengths we went to to wake him without making him lose his centre of gravity: stage whispers, pea shooters from the flies, splashes of cold water from the boys on the gantry. In the end we gave up and just dropped him. He stumbled to his feet, recited the opening verbatim and then staggered off in his 8-in heels muttering, 'Where's me bloody heart tablet.'

But worse, much worse, was imminent. Again the cause was an over-enthusiastic comic who thought he knew it all. There before me sat a full house of 1700 youngsters whose minders had blissfully dumped them in our care and retired for R and R. Each child had come equipped for the fray – blowers, streamers, balloons, sweets, chocolates, oranges, ice creams – enough to stave off the longest siege and still leave plenty of ammunition for assaulting the stage.

'Hello, children,' I trilled cheerily.

'Buzz, squawk, zoo-zoo,' came the chorus of party blowers and kazoos.

'We're going to have a great time today,' I persevered, though I didn't believe a word of it.

'Double Buzz, double squawk, double zoo,' they replied.

I've got to get these kids on my side, I thought desperately. I must appeal to their logic and reason.

'Very shortly, kids, the giant's coming on and he's very naughty. Will you boo him for me?'

A chorus of 'Yes, mister.' (Phew! Thank the Lord for that at least.)

'It's us against the giant then,' I stressed.

'All right, mister,' they promised, the fiends. So off I strode, little appreciating the fuse I'd lit.

On came the giant – eight feet tall in the built-up boots, ugly as sin, and bellowing through a radio mike:

'Fee, fi, fo, fum.'

As if one man, the audience showered the stage with a hail of Smarties and jelly beans, orange peel bounced off the footlights, and ice cream splattered the eight-foot frame of the giant, who called it quits and hobbled off stage.

'I'm not coming on again,' he whinged.

'But they're only kids,' I reasoned.

'It's like a battlefield out there. I'm an actor, and I'm not equipped for this.'

Off he lumbered to the safety of a locked dressing room, where he made running repairs with a bottle of Cyprus sherry.

'We've got to shut them up,' screamed Ronnie above the uproar.

'Send the dancing girls on. Show them a bit of leg.'

Hopeless, hopeless indeed, to expect glamour to impress the banshees out front. On went the girls, dancing a little, and slipping on the sweets a lot: bodies and legs everywhere, it resembled the roughest bar fight in the worst western movie.

'You started this,' glowered Ronnie at me. 'Get on and shut them up.'

'What'll I do?'

'Do the ghost routine. That'll slow them down.'

So on I went to run through the ancient routine of pacing the stage and being dogged by a dancer dressed in a sheet.

'Ghost,' screamed 1700 voices.

'Where?' I demanded.

'Behind you,' they chorused.

At this I performed the slow turn so that the ghost could keep behind my back.

'No, it isn't.'

'Yes, it is.'

'No, it isn't,' I persisted.

'Yes, it is,' they insisted.

I'd done this about six times when my gaze fell on a six-year-old girl and her younger brother in the front row. She looked at me disgustedly and turned to her brother: 'Henry, don't shout again, the man is obviously an idiot.'

Exit, pursued by a sheet.

13

When my Pat was a teenager she was told by a fortuneteller that she would never be rich but that 'as one door closes, another will open'. I don't believe that even the fortuneteller could have foreseen the accuracy of that prophecy. Over the years the O'Connor clan have known numerous places of residence, and they've included flats, maisonettes, semi- and detached houses, bungalows, three-storey homes and even a mobile home. At one point it became almost impossible to remember where my clothes were. Here? There? Or up the Great North Road doing a steady 70 mph. A lot of it could be blamed on the Inland Revenue, but I'll get to that anon. Meantime, let's pick up the threads of the family side of things and go from there.

Bearing in mind that we had two houses at the same time, Southport and Sandhurst, it now seems a little strange for us to have purchased a motorised camper, but it was one of those things that seemed like a good idea at the time. It had four berths, and was equipped with kitchen (with fridge, cooker and running water), dining and lounge areas and a chemical toilet. It appeared to be the answer to the entertainer's prayer. It had a top speed of 80 mph plus, was quite economical to run, easy to park, and could be powered by any one of three sources – spare battery, Calor gas or mains electric. What could have been better for the man on tour?

Well, one thing that could have been better was that when the thing was moving all the cutlery, china and glassware rattled like hell. It sounded like the old curiosity shop on wheels. Cornering became a manoeuvre full of dread, because that was when cupboards flew open and various items of foodstuff and personal belongings spilled out and bounced around the van. Pat's personal hell was the thought of anybody using the chemical loo. 'First one who goes on it cleans it out!' she insisted. Consequently, it was never used – even after Tommy Leddy assured us that, according to a mate of his, the van could be positioned over a grid in the street and the loo emptied out.

Whatever, the van had to go, even though it had proved the perfect base when I was working just a week or so at a venue. But it reminded me of a saying of W C Fields: 'Women are like fire engines. Everyone likes to see one, nobody wants to own one.'

I loved its comfort and luxury when it was stationary but its determination to spill every utensil, item of cutlery and anything else not nailed down meant it had to go. The family pondered other ways of spreading itself throughout the British Isles. London was the big lure in the later 1970s and '80s for two reasons. First, nearly all my TV work was based in or near the capital; and, second, more importantly, the club scene up north was changing and the recession was beginning to hit hard. Phones in agents' offices stopped ringing; acts that couldn't adapt were gradually phased out of the business. No longer were summer seasons, pantomimes and weeks in nightclubs the norm; indeed, they became the exception. Corporate work, after-dinner speaking, pro-celebrity golf days – these were avenues opening up for the comic. Touring game shows, a willingness to drive up to 2000 miles per week, and if necessary to lower fees – all these measures and more were needed if one was to stay in work. Adapt or die was the watchword. When recession bit, it always bit fiercer in the north than in the south. So go south, take the family and hope that luck will be kind to us. Swiss family O'Connor, off to the smoke. Well, Ascot actually: near enough, but also far enough away when it suited.

In those heady days of 1980, there was no thought in my head of selling either property we owned. Money was coming in and we were spending very little of it. As a bonus, the tax man was refusing to let me pay him! You don't get that happening too often; but more of that later. Suffice to say for now that I had plenty of spare dosh, so Pat set off on a hunt for more property. She found it in a lovely forest in Royal Ascot and the deal was done in no time. A beautiful cottage, acres of land, and not a lot to be done to bring it round to our way of living. In those days it was possible to drive from one's door to Marble Arch in 30 minutes. (Today it can take up to two hours, but we must have progress, you see.)

As with all dreams, or dream houses, they are made all the sweeter by having to endure the odd nightmare experience, and ours began at Ascot even before we had moved in. Psychologists reckon that moving house is one of the most traumatic experiences. They should try moving to a house under water. I did and lived to tell the tale.

By sheer good fortune, Pat had made friends with the housekeeper of the property next door. Lovely 'Jacko', a hard working, jolly Scotsman, had made a note of our Southport phone number and called us with the news that there was a major leak at Ascot. It seems that a lady from the local Neighbourhood Watch group had called round to welcome us, looked through the letter box of the empty cottage, and spotted water cascading down the stairs. A major extension had been added to the original building and a water pipe connecting the two sections had not been plumbed in properly. Result: Niagara Falls. I drove down from Liverpool post haste and started to mop up. Being an expert on ceilings damaged by water (remember our Hornby

Road house?), it was obvious to me that professional help was needed. Fortunately it was at a time when workmen not only agreed to do a job but actually turned up! Those days have long since gone in the Ascot area, but they are a happy memory.

So here was the comedian, living in a drying out house, listening to the hammering and sawing of a dozen artisans, and trying to picture a day when the roof stopped falling in on me. In truth, that blessed day just seemed to recede into the distance. Hardly was the lath and plaster dry on the ceilings than the good lord sent us gale-force winds and a 60-foot tree snapped and crashed through the roof. This resulted in the entire dismantling of one side of the house and many thousands of pounds worth of rebuilding. Hey, ho! I never had these problems with the mobile home. (On the other hand you didn't have to station the Ascot house over a road grid at loo times.)

It was all worth it in the long run. A peaceful setting, room to expand, a snooker room, all mod cons and friendly neighbours – what could be better? Even the postman became a personal friend. Letters addressed 'Tom O'Connor – Near London' were delivered without any problem. Occasionally they would be accompanied by a note, such as: 'Hope this means you'll stop taking the mickey out of the Post Office. Love, Postie.' To be honest I've never given the Post Office anything less than the highest praise, except in my 'no stamp' routine. Praise of sorts anyway. Basically the gag is that in order to have a letter delivered on time with no messing about, the idea is not to use a stamp at all. Instead on one side of the envelope you write a completely fictitious name and address. Then on the other side you write, 'If undelivered, please return to...' and the address you want the letter to go to. Sorry, postie. Won't do it again.

Known now as the land baron, it behoved me gradually to ease the family out of the north and lure them south before the showbiz bubble burst (the ever-pessimistic side of my comic's nature was always lurking just below the surface, despite the major offers and new TV series that were coming through). One by one, exams permitting, the children made their way to our new abode, settling either in jobs or, in the case of young Helen, in a new school. Typical of our peculiar way of doing things she chose to be a boarder at the Marist Convent, which was every inch of $1\frac{1}{2}$ miles from our front door. It enabled us to visit her while out shopping, or calling in at the local! Ah – and what a local!

The Cannon pub, situated on the main drag from Wentworth to Ascot, is a fine establishment with a special clientele – friendly, jocular, and all masters of the one-armed bandit. The owner until recently, Paul Styles, and his wife Audrey became two of our earliest and best friends. Their personalities and excellent home cooking ensured a full house almost every night, and almost full at lunchtime. Always a big draw on race days, the pub suddenly got an unexpected boost when an Arab neighbour decided to refurbish. Well to tell you the truth 'refurbish' hardly fits the bill. He'd bought the place for a mere £5 million and decided it needed 'doing up'. Well, you would, wouldn't you? A bomb-proof wall, a million bricks, sunken swimming pool, fall-out shelter – you name it, he specified it. 'Road-up' signs, traffic cones, drills, piles of bricks, mountains of sand – they all served to clutter, and often block, the road around the Cannon. It was bad for passing trade, but more than compensated for by the thirsty workmen who left the site at noon and drank till two.

The bulk of the workers were from the London area and the pub would resound to cockney voices and cockney humour. And then one day, totally out of the blue, I had that wonderful experience of hearing my own 'tongue' being spoken across a crowded room. It was one of those moments when the whole place goes quiet and you can pick out a familiar twang. The stranger was six foot tall, hairy, ugly, and build like the Wigan second row (I mean both of them). His voice boomed across the bar – 'Pint of bitter la.'

'Hey, you're a Scouse!' I remarked.

'That's right.'

'Are you working next door on the site?'

'Now, wish I was. I'm redundant. Been working abroad and got the sack,' he sighed.

'Oil rigs?' I suggested.

'Vatican,' he smiled.

'*Vatican*? Like the one in Rome?' I stuttered, little realising I was being led into a classic gag.

'Yeah. I was a tour guide and they sacked me.'

'What – they sacked you? What for?' I asked, eyes bulging. (God knows, I was the perfect straight man.)

'Well, I was showing a party around St Peter's and I was saying what a lovely person the Holy Father was. Just then, the Pope came round the corner and I said: "Oh, look! Talk of the devil!"'

Congratulations Scouse, you did me up like a kipper, much to the enjoyment of Paul, Audrey and all and sundry. Well, the drinks were on me. Not, incidentally, that I ever drink much, in pubs or elsewhere. Many an entertainer has fallen foul of alcohol and got into the ultimate 'Catch 22' of having to have a drink in order to go on then having to carry on drinking because the punters are treating you to glasses of your favourite; then sleeping on a skinful, rising hung over, and needing a 'hair of the dog' to restart the motor. With the odd exception I've managed to avoid having too much to drink, and thank God have never needed one to go on stage. It doesn't mean I've totally escaped the hospitality of the public – probably I've suffered worse than most on occasions. It's difficult to refuse a drink from a passing acquaintance who would like to return the snifter you bought him last time. You bite the bullet and sup anything they buy. This can be hard on the constitution if the bar is full of people all trying to buy you a jar. It's what you call a night for falling down.

Anyway, by every means possible Ascot welcomed us to its heart – even to its golf club. One day, I found myself paying the £4.50 green fee (I will say that again: £4.50 green fee – boy how times have changed) to play at Royal Ascot golf club. A super course, situated inside the beautiful race course on Ascot Heath. Being a fairish golfer, I found it a challenging eighteen holes, but I had a decent round and worked up a fierce thirst. Having quaffed a couple of pints I was leaving when the secretary Dennis Healey (no, not *that* Denis Healey) approached me.

What a shame that I was busy that evening, he said, because it was Captain's Night and they were short of a guest celebrity. No shame, Mr Secretary, and no problem. In fact, I was free that evening and it would be my pleasure to fill the gap. So began my relationship with a great group of lads and lasses. To start with, John O'Neill, the captain, happened to be the chairman of the club. He soon became, and he remains, my very best friend. Canny golfer, the most genial of companions and the truest of friends, this exiled Irishman and I have spent many long hours on golf courses (and their extremities) and also on motorways – for when he can, John operates as my aide-de-camp and Mr Fixit. He is not a perfect human being – I mean, the poor fellow has the most disgraceful golf swing – but is undoubtedly the perfect pal.

So here, since 1980, the family has lived and laughed. But what of our other residence? Well, let's get back to that matter of the Inland Revenue. It all begins with a taxman losing his job by the process mega-employers like to call 'natural wastage'. Whoever the bod was who was responsible for my particular affairs had had a bee in his bonnet for many years apparently. When he 'naturally wasted' he left a note in my file which his successor had to act upon. It involved the rights and wrongs of limited companies and their directors. In those days the rate of tax could be amazingly high depending on status, and companies paid less. Directors reaped benefits, but were stringently bound by certain rules. In theory, any member of the board could sign contracts, but my revenue chap wondered why only my name appeared on mine. Why couldn't Pat, as secretary, sign the document? My answer was simple. The rules governing artistes' contracts stated that the entertainer should 'sign as known'. In other words Dana should sign 'Dana' and not her real name, Rosemary Brown. The same applied to Lulu and Englebert Humperdink.

After a couple of days of explaining the various 'ins', 'outs' and 'isms' of showbusiness, the matter was passed on to two presiding judges, who ruled in my favour. I think what swung it for me was the opposition's production of a contract which I had signed 'Tom O'Connor'. On reading it fully we all realised that the venue had signed itself not by the owner's name but 'Chicken in the Basket'. This brought gales of laughter. As I prepared to leave the witness box, my heart sank as one of the judges said:

'One last question, Mr O'Connor.'

'Oh! Oh!' I thought.

'What did you think of Jimmy O'Dea?' he enquired.

'A fine comedian, my lord,' I owned up truthfully. 'His act still gets laughs – ask Frank Carson!'

So the problem of tax was solved, but now I had to pay a five-year tax bill. This I did by selling our place at Sandhurst, and dispatching the full amount to the Revenue. However, the house price exceeded the tax owed by several thousand pounds. Where would I like the balance returned? Nowhere, I said: keep it against future demands and meantime invest it at the highest rate of interest that can possibly be found. This shook my pal at the Revenue, but it was the law. Surprising what you can learn from a retired accountant over a pint at Royal Ascot Golf Club! To conclude this little episode, let me quote the brilliant line attributed to Ken

Dodd on the night he won his tax case. Walking on to a packed house, and before saying 'good evening', Doddy said:

'Two hundred years ago a man invented income tax. He started at three pence in the pound – nobody told me he'd changed it!'

14

So far in my account of my progress on stage and TV I've concentrated on those in front of the audience and those whose obvious talents are listed in credits at the end of the show. But what of the forgotten men and women of showbusiness. For instance, what of hairdressers? I'm lucky because my daughter Helen provides that service – better than any other I've known (OK, so I'm a little biased). What of accountants? In John Bradney I've certainly struck oil, and his 'oppo' John Westlake sees to it that my money is well invested. Legally, I have found the finest and best: dear Henri Brandman, my friend and my best gag finder. So far so good. The act, the monetary security, the coiffure, but what about the clothes?

There's an old adage that goes: 'If you're going to talk money, you've got to look money.'

I always look at my best thanks to Robbie Stanford – the number one of all London tailors. Robbie's style and cut make an artiste stand out in any crowd. Bob Monkhouse, Englebert, Tom Jones – even me! Though of all his many sartorially elegant clients, only I have been fitted for a pair of trousers in the doorway of Watford town hall at 2 am.

Because of our mutual schedules it was virtually impossible to meet in more suitable premises, and so the venue had to be Watford on a foggy night. Thank God no policeman saw the huddled twosome, one with coat collar raised to assist anonymity, the other cheerily taking an inside leg measurement as if it were the most natural thing to do! It seems we always meet in strange fitting rooms – lifts, hotel bedrooms – yes, even a mobile home clattering to the sound of cutlery. Wherever and whenever, the results have always been excellent and on many an occasion been the final brick in the wall when my name has been selected for a specific job.

It certainly swung it for me when a BBC producer came to see my show in Blackpool. Dear Alan Walsh (God rest you, sir) was taken with my appearance and offered me the position of host for a brand new series called *A Question of Entertainment*. Based on the ratings winner *A Question of Sport*, it featured two teams of celebrities answering queries on the world of showbusiness, past and present. As a compère job it was dead easy, made more so by the talents of the team captains, Ken Dodd and Larry Grayson. Two men who'd been there, done that, seen everything and were fazed by nought. The only drawback to the show was the time limit: many's the time we recorded over an hour for the half-hour programme. What I would give to see the out-takes! We three recorded only one series, but happily the show lives on under another name, *That's Showbusiness*. It's good that such a great format should remain as an epitaph to that good man, Alan Walsh.

While the door of the BBC was closing on the O'Connors, the ITV door re-opened at Tyne Tees, where they needed a presenter for a crossword-puzzle game called *Cross Wits*. If *Name That Tune* was ideal for an ex-music teacher, then *Cross Wits* was even more so for a lover of word puzzles of every kind. Four, sometimes five newspapers a day fail to quench my thirst for crosswords; books of puzzles also litter our house. If the gods of luck had asked me to choose but one show to host in all my years I would not have chosen any other than *Cross Wits*. Simple format (always a key to success), audience participation (vital for a popular quiz), goodish prizes, and a genuine requirement of skill and knowledge. (I detest those shows where it's possible to win a car just for knowing your own name.)

No matter how many other attributes can be listed in favour of this show, let me describe the particular things I liked when taking the reins. To begin with the venue is Newcastle, home of hard-working people of ready wit, tremendous loyalty and gentle nature. It's always a pleasure to be among these folk who've known more bad times than good in economic terms, but who still smile with a genuine happiness. No task is too difficult for my production crew, no burden too heavy for them to bear. To make it even better, a majority of the crew are ladies – researchers, make-up, production assistants – always a big help because, unlike men, the ladies will forever call a spade a spade and admit culpability when mistakes are made. But at the top of the proceedings I'm grateful for the presence of my favourite producer of all, Christine Williams. Chris looks after the whole shebang as if it were her own personal possession. It might as well be because she knows its every part and loves it with great passion. A great moulder of personalities, Chris has the gift of making every good idea appear to be yours and yet possesses the firmness to accept any or all the blame if ideas are found to be duds. Bless you, Chris, you've nursed this old frame of mine through many a hard time and kept me going with cheerfulness and encouragement. (You've also been responsible for fattening my frame with too much good grub over the past nine series. At least a stone a time is the average, so now I've had to go on a strict diet after each recording session.)

'You look an awful lot thinner than you do on telly,' say the little old ladies. 'It must be the lighting.' If only you knew, girls.

And so the role of game-show host continues, as does my 'real' job of comedian and reporter on life. It never ceases to amaze me how many new avenues can open up when all seems to have been achieved. Who'd have thought that the docker's lad from Liverpool would end up talking to audiences all over the world? Who'd have thought they'd have bothered to listen? Maybe they wouldn't if I had not got lucky once again. It was back to ships and cruises that gave me the chance to perform in front of many nationalities all gathered together. It may sound daunting, but in fact it is a lot easier than working to a room full of drunks.

P&O have made it possible for Pat and me to see the world and talk to its people. Oh, yes, I've had to work my passage, but that's nothing compared to the sights we've seen and the memories we have. Each year from 1979 onwards we've been lucky enough to join either the *Canberra* or *Sea Princess* on a leg of the world cruise and sail two or three weeks to ports of our choosing in the merriest of company. There's surely no better gathering of folk than those out to enjoy themselves and relax under the sun. And what an audience! People from all walks of life sharing the same floating hotel. A city at sea, emptying at each port and then refilling at a designated time and moving on to another ocean, another country. Over the years we've grown accustomed to life aboard and the problems besetting passengers and crew alike. Generally they can be put down to simple misunderstandings and can be solved with a little thought.

Take the old lady who came aboard at Southampton, went to her cabin after lunch – and disappeared for over two days. Admittedly the weather was bad through the Bay of Biscay, but still you'd think she'd have shown herself if only to get some fresh air. Worried folk from her restaurant table alerted the crew, who hastened to her cabin only to find the door unlocked and the lady sitting distraught on her bed.

'Thank God you've come – I've been stuck here for two days,' she sobbed.

'Well, why didn't you open the door?' asked the sailors.

'I did, but all that was on the other side was a bathroom.'

'But why didn't you open the other door?' they asked.

'Well, I didn't like to because it had "Do not disturb" on the door handle,' she explained. Silly? Stranger things happen at sea. Take the well-to-do gent that I met in the bar one evening after a piano recital. He and I talked of this and that – sport, and finance, and how to put the world to rights. After a couple of jars we were joined by his wife, a charming person whom I'd seen on many occasions while passing through the slot machine arcade. She was always there; she seemed obsessed by the spinning reels of cherries, bars and oranges. I didn't want to refer to what appeared to be her gambling obsession, but she came right out with it.

'It's a change to see me away from fruit machines, I suppose?'

'Well, yes,' said I.

'She spends all her time there,' said her husband. 'She gets through about 300 quid a day.'

'Wow,' I mused. 'Wouldn't it be cheaper to buy a machine of your own and leave it in your cabin?'

'Good heavens no, old chap,' he boomed. 'She'd never be out from under my feet!'

Well, there's proof that there are things more important than money – as long as you have lots of money, that is.

Not all those who cruise are oddballs; quite the contrary. Here you meet people who have found what for them is the greatest form of relaxation and throw themselves whole-heartedly into all that is on offer. Swimming (on board of course), golf (in nets naturally), deck quoits, deck tennis, jogging, walking, keep fit, dancing, quizzes, handicrafts – they're all there for the asking. Peaceful pursuits by day, and dancing, cabaret and audience participation at night.

A new port every other day or so, then off we go again. Even as a hired hand with a certain amount of work to do, I find the whole set-up the most perfect way of reducing blood pressure and easing stress. Far away from the cares of the world and the blare of the tabloids, it's amazing how little one misses out on. It's remarkable how little the world changes in the fourteen or so days without direct contact.

But, on water as on land, there's no fool like an old fool – and there's no old fool like old T O'Connor. I fall into a trap, swear never to do it again, and then forget my oath. Consider the matter of the biscuits.

Every cabin has a steward whose task it is to look after the creature comforts of the passengers, including room service. It's always nice to ring through for a pot of tea or coffee, and the beverage is generally accompanied by a couple of packs of biscuits per person. Many's a time there is no space in one's stomach for food, but, rather than leave the snacks on the tray for removal, I tend to shove them in a drawer for consumption another time. The trouble is, 'another time' never comes and the drawer gets fuller, till the fortnight ends with an embarrassed comic trying to stuff two hundredweight of McVities' finest in his hand luggage rather than upset the steward.

My life-long pal Frank Travers and I met when he was working on our cabin block. A cheery soul, Frank, whistling all the time and never anything but extremely happy. We've shared some great times aboard and ashore. I mean, what about Yokohama? Frank, Pat, Ray Allen the ventriloquist and I went exploring the dockland area of the Japanese port and ended up in the type of pub you see in black-and-white eastern movies. It was full of sailors from Russia and Britain and enhanced (if that's the word I'm groping for) by the presence of three ladies of questionable age but unquestionable purpose. Straight out of the 1930's epic *Shanghai Lil* they vamped the beer-laden sailors with a species of roguish charm that would have curdled milk. It was quite obvious even to our landlubbers' eyes that trouble was a-brewing. After 20 minutes we supped up and left – just in time. I can't remember what came through the window

first – a chair or Shanghai Lil. The battle of all time raged
in the pub before the Japanese police arrived, batons drawn,
and locked up everybody! What a story we'd have had to
tell if it had started 20 minutes earlier, but Frank had seen
the danger and had got us out before the fur began to fly.

No stranger to danger, our Frank. Not a big man in build,
but a giant in character. He was first to volunteer when the
bugle blew. Bugle? Yes, in 1982, when the Falklands war
broke out. *Canberra* was needed as a troopship, and every
single member of the crew elected to serve. It had all started
so peculiarly – you'd never have thought there was a
war on. *Canberra* was returning to Southampton from the
Seychelles. We were supposed to pick up an illusionist called
Graham P Jolley at one of the ports. Poor Graham: first we
missed out Malta, then he tried to join us at Naples and
missed the boat; he finally caught up with us at Gibraltar.
By now it was known that the ship would be making the
long journey to war and had to lose no time getting home
for a refit. We had a navy admiral and several SAS men to
pick up on the way, which bothered me none except that
they decided to come on board during my cabaret act! We
were passing Gibraltar and I sat in the dressing room waiting
to go on – when suddenly the ship stopped. Yes, stopped –
just like that! Normally a big ship like that needs some
distance to glide to a halt. This time she just stopped. What
was going on? The passengers ran to the side of the ship
and saw our unscheduled new arrivals suspended down the
side to a launch bouncing about below. One old dear,
peering down from the promenade deck, turned to her
neighbour and said: 'I think it's disgraceful that first class
passengers have to board in this way.'

Anyway, the new arrivals were safely installed – as was
Graham P Jolley, who managed to get in one show before
we reached Southampton. There everyone was hurriedly
disembarked and the ship made ready for war. I left one
thought with the crew on a last-night show in their mess.

'Wait till tomorrow. There'll be thousands of people lining the quayside waving and cheering 'cos they're *not* going' – it made them smile. It also prompted them to leave me with the unenviable task of informing their families that they'd volunteered to go to war. 'Ring this number after we sail, and explain,' I was asked at least a dozen times. I did ring and I did explain, and I soon had the feeling that I was becoming the most unpopular comic in Britain. Still, they all went, and thank God they all returned. They took an army half way across the world and never lost a man. It made me tearfully proud to have been associated with them.

Perhaps I'm a latter-day Jonah, but I've been on board on several occasions when crises or potential disasters have loomed. I was doing my stint aboard *Sea Princess* when it was involved in the *Ocean Pearl* incident. That cruise ship was ablaze and drifting in the Indian Ocean when our captain was signalled that his was the nearest vessel. He immediately set course for the *Ocean Pearl*, hoping to arrive in time to rescue at least some passengers and crew. As we approached we could see huge flames and smoke pouring out of the stricken vessel.

Calm as you like, but ever so efficiently, our boats made the round trip to the *Ocean Pearl* and transferred everyone, luggage and all, to *Sea Princess*. What a celebration we had! What a night! We found room to bunk every newcomer, and I put on a special show for them. Imagine the reception I got from the mostly American audience – it seemed we'd never stop the merriment. Afterwards, a very nice Yank said to me:

'What about if I give you a gag you've never heard? Would that show our appreciation?'

'Certainly,' I said, and he gave me the latest Bill Clinton story – maybe you've heard it now, but it was brand new at the time.

President Clinton and Hillary were out driving and they

stopped for petrol. As the attendant pumped the gas, Hillary Clinton said:

'Hey, I know this guy.'

'Really,' said Bill.

'Yes. I was at college with him years ago. In fact, I was engaged to him before I married you.'

'Well, there you are,' said Bill. 'If you hadn't changed your mind, you'd be married to a petrol attendant.'

'No,' smiled Hillary. 'If I hadn't changed my mind – *he'd* be the president!'

So now I was getting jokes from Americans and retelling them to Australians, New Zealanders, South Africans – in fact anyone who could speak the language. Mixed audiences really are easy if they'll listen. They've all got the same little foibles – fear of flying, trouble with the in-laws, the propensity to say ridiculous things:

'Sorry I'm late, I had to go to the vet's – the cat's as sick as a dog!'

'Don't turn round but look who's behind you.'

The repertoire was building and the fame was spreading, eventually reaching Australia but not in the overnight rush of publicity – more in a slow and deliberate way.

When asked to name my favourite places, I always put Sydney at the top. It's a city buzzing with life, beauty, and expectation. Everybody seems to be going forward at a great rate of knots and all seems well even if it isn't. It's a great experience entering the harbour aboard a huge liner and sailing virtually into the city centre. My first visit coincided with the 200th anniversary of the arrival of the first settlers, and Pat and I had plenty of fun over a couple of days. We found a terrific pub called the Henry 9th at the foot of the Hilton Hotel. It seemed the entire pub was Irish, at least that's the impression we got as we were served Guinness in the street (the place was full to overflowing and we couldn't actually get inside). We could, however, hear a fine Irish group singing their own composition, 'Happy Birthday, dear old Dublin', a song I've never forgotten.

Three years later we were back in Sydney. This time we flew in to join *Canberra* on the Australia to Hong Kong leg of a cruise. We settled into our hotel and quickly sought out the Henry 9th. Sure enough, there was a group singing on stage. During their break I approached the lead singer, Myles Mooney, and discovered he had written that memorable song. Would the boys do it for me? Certainly they would, and they gave me a copy of their record. We had a few jars that night and talked of things, mostly of Ireland and Dublin in particular. The boys were delighted that I knew a lot of the songs they sang, little knowing that years before I'd sung them myself in Liverpool's Irish Centre.

Next day I was booked to appear on a live chat-cum-light entertainment programme – the *Ray Martin Show*. I followed the lovely Tammy Wynette and chatted generally to Ray about my career, peppering it with gags and true stories.

'Where were you last night?' asked Ray.

'Henry 9th. Great night and if the Irish Drovers are watching – thanks, fellas.'

The Drovers *were* watching that night and were waiting for me.

'You never told us you were famous,' they said.

'You never asked, and anyway so what?'

'Agreed,' said Myles, and with that we laid into the Guinness and Jameson's. I just made the ship in time before she sailed. I remember little of the day except the very nicest of feelings.

I played the Drovers' record till it virtually wore out. I dream of one day returning and perhaps performing in Sydney Opera House with the boys on as my special guests. Only a dream so far, but who knows what can happen with the luck of the Irish.

Ah, yes – and what about the Irish?

15

The roots of my love affair with the Emerald Isle are deeply planted. Second generation Irish on both sides of the family, it was always our custom, nay duty, to visit Ireland every year during school holidays. There's hardly a place I haven't been to, seen, and (at least in the case of the Blarney Stone) kissed. From Cork to Donegal, from Dublin to Sligo, I've seen the forty shades of green – the greens that, like the shamrock, can be found only in that beautiful land. By family upbringing and by the years spent in and around Liverpool, I learned Irish ways of thinking, drinking and talking. Oh yes, they do talk their own way:

'Follow me. I'm right behind you.'

'You three are a right pair if ever I saw one!'

Nothing about Ireland surprises me any more.

It was in 1977 that I first went there to work. It was at a fine venue – Portmarnock Country Club. A week's cabaret, with accommodation and golf thrown in, and a chance to see the sights. The club even gave us a driver and car to take us around. We went to visit Pat's relatives, Auntie Bridie and family, near Mullingar. It was a pleasant enough drive on a winding road. On the way we chatted with our driver about the lack of motorways and the hope they'd soon be built. Soon would be fine for him – but it was too late for his pal Mick and his Jensen Interceptor. Mick had written the car off in the most bizarre circumstances imaginable. He was driving home one dark evening when towards him in the gloom he could see what appeared to be lights in the sky. As he got nearer, the lights seemed to be about twenty feet in the air and pointing down onto the road. It looked exactly as if a light plane was attempting to make an emergency landing on the road. With no time to think, Mick threw the wheel hard over. The car skidded off the road and crashed down into a ditch.

What of the plane? There was no plane. The oncoming lights were from a car transporter carrying six vehicles from Dublin docks. Apparently the truck's lights had failed and, to light the road, the driver had climbed up and put on the headlights of the first car on the upper deck of the trailer. What a mess. What a waste of a super car.

Still, a story to tell the folks back home – along with the conversation I had in a Dublin pub that week. On the wall they had a notice 'Appearing here tonight: the fabulous O'Rafferty Brothers.'

'Are they any good?' I enquired of the fella behind the bar.

'Sure, they're brilliant,' he enthused. 'We had them here once before and they never turned up!'

There didn't seem much more to be said on that subject, so I pointed to a headline in the local paper.

'What a terrible accident on the Naas road.'

'Oh, it was worse than terrible, sir. Eight people killed in a head-on collision. Eight people – and they were lucky!' he said.

'They were lucky?' I repeated.

'Yes, that there weren't more in the cars.'

Yes, of course – silly of me to ask.

So hello and welcome to Old Erin, land of miles of smiles, where time goes by and things get done, but not at any perceptible speed, and with a wonderful absence of stress. How I love the land and its people – the world's gentlefolk.

Until recently my visits have been restricted to Dublin and the north, but gradually my work is encompassing all the places I knew as a boy.

I suppose the breakthrough came while I was working at the Braemar Rooms, Dublin, for a couple of days. As the run included a Friday, I was invited onto the *Late, Late Show* and met and befriended the wonderful Gay Byrne. He let me joke, tell true tales and even sing a song called 'When I was a lad', accompanied by a multi-talented group of children called the Billy Barries. This show proved a springboard for me. It seems that everyone in Ireland watches it, and suddenly I was big news. One show led to another and another and even a fourth. In fact it's virtually a permanent date for me whenever I'm in town, thanks to the great man. I've plugged my two golf books on his show and watched them reach the best-seller lists (another impossible dream realised). I've also been able to mention the venues I was appearing at, with the result that the audiences turned out in force, and I now have a regular following.

It was at the Clontarf Castle, a great cabaret spot in Dublin, that I met lovely Jack, the man with the 'message'. No, not a divine message, but the code word for his favourite tipple – whiskey and red lemonade, would you believe. The late and much-mourned Jack Leonard was compère at the Castle for over 20 years. A talented pro who'd been booked for a week and then stayed on to run things, he was a legend years before I made his acquaintance. He was a lovely gentleman who had forgotten more about showbusiness than any three others of us will ever know. He put me right in all things to do with entertaining the Irish – the real folk, not the overseas visitors.

We shared a dressing room one week, and I watched his ritual of getting dressed and made up, getting briefed on the night's guest, and sorting out the 'message'. Everybody – management, staff and artistes – knew that Jack brought his own drink into the venue. It was cheaper, of course, and for the sake of decorum Jack would bring in two half bottles wrapped in brown paper bags and hidden on the floor under his make-up shelf. He'd buy a couple of legitimate whiskeys from the bar in order to obtain the glasses, and then for the rest of the night the 'message' would come out of the paper bags. That way he never knew how much he'd drunk until the two half bottles were empty. Well at least that was the story. His story ended sadly when the Lord took him away to a 'message in the sky'. There he sits in the heavenly dressing room, trying to kid the Guvnor that he's buying the house whiskey. Sorry to lose you, Jack – but you'd be proud of your successor. George Hunter, a fine compère and an even better singer. He's even a tasty golfer. He doesn't get the 'message' though. But he knows he's got a tough act to follow and he does it well.

Clontarf has been a home from home to me now for several years. At the same time it is a great place for me to try out new material. Believe me, if the lines don't work in Clontarf they won't work anywhere! Many's the night I'm still on stage after two hours' chat and have hardly noticed the passing of the time. The audiences are a comic's dream and the staff, led by lovely Ann D'Arcy, are the finest and the best. So congenial is it to work here that my best efforts are usually directed towards keeping everything on track and not wandering aimlessly through the myriad gags in the far corners of my brain. It gets to the point where Pat has to sit there with pen and paper lest I insert the odd new line and then can't remember it when the show's over.

And then, when the show is over, Ireland is the ideal place to unwind. All right, Scotland is the home of golf, but if ever there was a second home it must be the Emerald Isle. It seems that everybody, old, young, male or female is either a golfer or a close relative of one. All are eager to organise a knock for the journeyman comic, and there just aren't enough daylight hours to cope with the offers. My present ambition is to play at as many courses as I can when on tour, but whatever, I always reserve two or three days for St Margaret's Golf and Country Club, a marvellous newish complex near Dublin. Dennis Kane and the staff have become firm friends over the years and they can't wait to fill me in on the latest happenings. Like Tommy the bar manager, who was approached by two visiting English golfers:

'Excuse me – do you have a television lounge?'

'Yes, sir, through there.'

'And do you have Sky,' they enquired.

'Yes, up there, sir – there's acres of it,' explained your man.

It seems that every time I mention Ireland I'm reminded of a funny story. No fluke, I think, but more a tribute to the native wit of the folk, who can see the humorous side of all things even when under stress. North and south of the border I've been witness to many funnies, oddities, and cor-blimeys. Hardly anybody believes my account of my first visit to Belfast. Over flew Mr Cocky, Liverpool comic full of confidence and determined to take Ulster by storm. I was very swiftly brought down to earth by an event that left my best gags and flights of fantasy gasping for breath. While preparing to be interviewed at a Belfast radio station I was supping coffee and listening to the two o'clock news bulletin. One of the items was a report of a Dan Air plane that had been involved in a curious incident. Apparently the plane was circling Belfast Aldegrove airport when it disappeared off the radar screens.

'Where are you?' asked ground control.

'I'm down,' replied the pilot.

'No, you're not,' replied ground control.

'Believe me I am, and I should know,' insisted the skipper.

'Well, what can you see?'

'Cows and grass.'

'What?'

'Cows and grass, weeds, and ... oh, dear!'

It emerged that the plane had come down in a disused RAF landing strip a few miles from the airport. I suppose an easy mistake to make – but what about the implications? Firstly, there was not enough runway for the captain to take off again. Secondly, there were no steps to debark the passengers, so the emergency slides had to be fired and the folks requested to slip ungracefully to the ground. Bad enough already, but what of the baggage? Couldn't be unloaded in the absence of Customs officials. One had visions of a hundred irate punters chasing a frightened flight crew across a deserted air strip, howling for blood.

'Bit of a shambles,' I remarked to the radio interviewer.

'Ah yes, a little out of the ordinary,' he agreed.

'How will they rescue the plane?' I wondered.

'Sure, they'll take off the wings and tow it back to Aldergrove by road.' He then added the spine-tingling words: 'At least, that's what they did the last time!' For heaven's sake, I'd come here to make the people laugh. What chance had I?

The answer to that is that you can never predict the moment when your skills will be appreciated. The ways of God are wondrous in their timing and their power. And what I love about the Irish temperament is that it can ride over all things with a gentleness which casts out fear. It was Christmas, 1992, and Paul Elliott – that master-producer of pantomime – had asked me to appear at the Opera House, Belfast, in *Babes in the Wood*. My first opportunity to play a robber: a kind of semi-baddy as opposed to the friendly scamp of my former years. A good company, a fine script and a beautiful theatre: what more could one ask? Peace, Lord: give us peace. Sadly, it was a time of very heavy terrorist activity – an attempt to bring Belfast's business community to the very doors of the bankruptcy court. The effort failed, but it claimed many casualties on the way.

In hindsight it's easy to say that I should never have been booked into the Europa Hotel, the most bombed hostelry on earth. But it was so handy for the theatre – just a short stroll. Wasn't it Christmas, and wouldn't there be peace on earth and good will to all men? Fat chance! Day four of rehearsals found us homeless. A 1400 lb van bomb had blown up the hotel, my car, and sadly the backstage, business end of the beautiful Opera House. As the dust settled and the glass and rubble were being cleaned up the company was recalled to Britain, and all seemed over. That's what I thought, but then who was I to underestimate the spirit of the Ulster people. It began with a quiet approach from a very lovely person – Isabel Huddleston, owner of the Le Mons Hotel on the outskirts of Belfast. She had a large restaurant that she thought could be adapted to take a pantomime. Would I consider staying if we could put a show together? Certainly I would – but what about backup? Well, here's where the Lord played his aces. Present, willing and able were John Lenahan, a comedian who dresses as an Old Mother Riley character known as May McFetteridge and brings tears of laughter with the funniest act you'll ever see; Candy Divine, a fine singer and very popular radio presenter; and her husband Donald who undertook to ferret, cajole, bully and beseech all the help we needed. Sponsors suddenly came from nowhere: Calorgas, Telecom, Guinness – the names appeared as the lovely Francesca, my self appointed PA, noted what we needed and who would provide it. Radio microphones, speakers, lights – all the usual theatre paraphernalia needed to be obtained, transported and installed. Pat O'Kane and her volunteer crew from the Arts Theatre pitched in – and suddenly we seemed to have the makings of a show!

South of the border came to our aid in the form of costumes from the Gaiety Theatre, Dublin, and Fossetts Circus provided tiered seating and very, very talented speciality act. Together with our lovely little dancers and young man Paul Bloomer, all of eight years old, who would be Aladdin, the form of a 'real show' began to emerge. But what about the villain? If we were going to change the whole production to *Aladdin*, we'd need a good villain. Paul Elliott had kindly sent us scripts, music and so on – but good villains are born, not found in a stock cupboard. In a word, we needed John Hewitt, the man who would have played the Sheriff of Nottingham in the original show, who by now had resigned himself to spending Christmas out of work but raising the odd jar and enjoying 'the crack' in his native city of Belfast. No one knew his address. How were we going to find him?

No trouble – this is a land of infinite resourcefulness. We reasoned that he'd be drinking. He didn't drive, therefore he would at all times be within a very small distance of the city. So Candy Divine hit on the brilliant wheeze of using the local radio station to ask him to get in touch. 'If anyone is drinking with John Hewitt, will they stick him in a cab and send him to Le Mons, drunk or sober' was the message. It worked in no time. Our villain was found, the team was complete – and the show went on.

I was mainly an observer during all this frantically pro-ductive to-ing and fro-ing. I still wonder at the strength of character of those people. It was as if the whole province had decided to prove that violence would not be permitted to prevail and that Christmas would not be blown away. We had a terrific time, a panto that gradually grew from a scrabbled playlet into a half-decent production and some unforgettable experiences. God forbid that you should ever be at the wrong end of a van bomb. But it you are, try to remember what you think of and what you try to rescue in the scramble to safety. I managed to grab my mobile phone as Pat and I ran to safety. Pat, for some reason known only to herself, managed to leave behind all the basic necessities of woman kind: no purse, no handbag, no hair rollers. No, she just grabbed a cheque made out to Barclaycard.

Pat's order of priorities amused my managers, Tommy and Kevin, when they came over to view the opening night of our run. The Guinness people gave us the biggest bottle of champagne I'd ever seen, and we had a great time toasting all our team and the sponsors. That night we all slept the sleep of the just. Well, not quite all of us. Tommy was woken at some ungodly hour by the buzzing of an approaching motorbike. This got steadily louder and louder until it seemed to be right underneath his window. Could it be a terrorist bomber? They were known to travel on motorbikes for quick getaways. Should he rouse everybody, running the risk of being made to look a fool if it were a false alarm? Finally, being British, he decided that he'd rather die than make a fool of himself, and he just sat and stared out of the window – and watched the day-shift porter arrive and the night porter leave using the same bike!

The cast, crew, sponsors, patrons and children involved in that pantomime will always have a tale to tell. The press, TV and radio were brilliant. Without them we wouldn't have had a chance. Looking back with the comfort of a two year buffer, and a more peaceful period of my career, you might think I would have only amusing memories of those days. And that's mostly true – but what lingers most powerfully in my mind to this day is the moment I had with two small kids. In order to flesh out our show into two solid hours, and because we lacked much of the glitter and glam of a normal theatre show, we had to adapt. So, with the help of young volunteers from the audience, I played a potted version of *Name That Tune* and gave away prizes and sweets.

On the opening night I asked for two youngsters to come on stage. The place was so full of atmosphere that I swear if you had touched a wall you'd have received an electric shock. My daughter Anne Marie, who was helping out with the choreography, had positioned a couple of helpers to lead the kids up. So I stood between these two five-year-old contestants, ribbed them gently, and 'persuaded' them into guessing the titles of various carols. But then came the

crunch. Have you ever had a day when the mouth won't
work properly? As the two were about to leave the stage,
they turned to me and said: 'Thanks for staying.'

I was completely pole-axed. And as tears filled my eyes,
I could tell them nothing less than the truth: 'But I'd nowhere
else to go.'

And, years later, let me say, there's nowhere else I'd rather
have been.

16

Throughout these scribblings I've been aware that there's a whole raft of rather special experiences that need to be fitted in somehow. So here, cheek by jowl, are a few of the ones that will remain in my memory for ever.

Let me start with my Princess Anne story. It was a gala evening at Woolwich Arsenal barracks in aid of the Army Benevolent Fund. The guest of honour was Her Royal Highness and the celebrities included Ernie Wise, Angela Rippon and names from every corner of *Who's Who*. The cabaret was to feature young Katy Budd, a lovely lady with a terrific act, and yours truly. Before the whole event it was our pleasure to meet and chat with the princess. The weather is always a good topic for openers, so there we stood bemoaning the fog that was descending outside.

'Totally scuppers tomorrow if I'm not careful,' said Princess Anne.

'Why's that, Ma'am?' I asked.

'I've got to be in Swindon tomorrow for some horse trials, and there's talk of my helicopter being stranded here with fog.'

'What a shame,' said I. 'Wish I could help.' (Looking back I realise I never should have said those words.)

'Maybe you can,' said the princess. 'You live in Ascot, don't you?'

'Er – yes, Ma'am,' I mumbled.

'Well, that's on the way. We could stay the night at your place!' She smiled happily.

I can't read royal faces very well and to this day I'll never know if she was joking or not. But suppose she wasn't. How could I ring home and tell my dad to wake the kids and reshuffle the sleeping arrangements.

'Just find a good reason to refuse,' said her bodyguard, apparently more worried than me.

'But it's a Royal Command,' I said despairingly.

I spent one of the longest nights of my life at that 'do'. All the time I was on stage I prayed for the fog to lift. It did, thank goodness. But I was a nervous wreck for several days afterwards. Eventually I got over it, and settled for an imposing plaque in our bedroom: 'Princess Anne never slept here.'

Unforgettable moments are like fine wines, they improve with age. It feels as if this next tale has been with me a hundred years, but that can't be true. The players, the scenario, the walk-ons, were all surely cast in heaven, if heaven is where laughter originates.

Pat and I were aboard the beautiful *QE2*, where I was helping to entertain a full complement of passengers enjoying a cruise to the Canary Islands and back. Sponsored by *TV Times*, the trip was full of well-organised events and featured many celebrities. Among them were our good friends Bert and Maggie Weedon (ah, Bert – you're still my all-time favourite guitarist) and another happy couple, Iris Williams, the beautiful Welsh songstress, and her then husband Clive Brandy. An amazing man, Clive. Abandoned by the act he was managing while on a tour of Australia, he was left penniless and in the direst of straits. But, typically of the man, he bounced around working where he could, being a comic or a compère or anything that would earn a crust, working the toughest of the tough clubs and at stockyards in the Outback. He even managed to get aboard an England-bound freighter and worked his passage back to Southampton. On disembarkation it suddenly dawned on him that if he could get to London for free he'd have travelled halfway across the world for nothing. And so he pulled the old con trick with the rail ticket. You've heard of it in jokes, you've seen it in comedy films: Clive Brandy did it in real life out of sheer desperation.

Boarding a London-bound train, he gambled that somewhere along the way someone would need to go to the loo, so he positioned himself near a toilet and waited. Sure enough, along came a chap answering nature's call. He had locked himself inside and was allowing nature to take its course when there was a peremptory knock on the loo door.

'Tickets, please.'

'But, but . . .'

'No buts, sir – please slide your ticket under the door.'

'Oh, very well,' came a resigned muttering from inside, and in a moment the ticket appeared.

'Thank you, sir,' said Clive, and scarpered to the other end of the train. What an evil fellow!

So, back to the *QE2* and our return from Madeira. En route we were told there was a dock strike at home and we were diverting to Cherbourg. Ever aware that the best can always be made of a mess, we three married couples sat and plotted fun. Why not go to Paris for a few days and just relax where no one knew us? This might be our one and only chance to stay at the magnificent George V hotel. It would be a sin not to take it. So off we went by express train (fully ticketed, I might add) to Gay Paree. The journey was spent in the bar amongst the most incredible characters none of whom spoke a word of English – not even Scouse. According to Clive, who performed his own version of 'Give us a clue', they were ex-members of the French resistance movement returning from a reunion and reminiscing over the good old desperate days. They were in fits of laughter, which gave way to songs – in which we joined – amazing how happiness is contagious. By the time we got to Paris we'd had a series of amazing conversations with the Frenchmen – you've no idea how riotously noisy mime can be – and we had put the world to rights. But that was only the start of the fun.

Three days and nights we six enjoyed in the city of love. We wondered at the sights, we drooled at the food, we fell in love with the city and pulled it on us like a favourite jumper. One feature of Parisian nightlife that makes me return year after year is the fantastic cabaret circuit – the Moulin Rouge, Crazy Horse, Lido, *et al*. They are second to none in their splendour and their content. The very best magicians, ventriloquists, dancers, singers (language is no barrier here): total enjoyment is the aim. And we were out for total enjoyment that night at the Crazy Horse. That night when for a split second the world stopped spinning and I left my earthly form, rose up, and looked down at myself and my company.

Don't worry – it wasn't that freaky. It was merely a matter of getting to grips with the situation. We six had chosen a table near the stage and ate and supped with gay abandon while waiting for the show to start. Around us sat Japanese tourists, too many to count, who had seen twenty countries that morning, videoed half of Europe and bought the rest. There they all sat, heads in the soup, fast asleep, while on stage pranced 16 beautiful dancers all totally naked – I mean, not a stitch! Shame the Japs were missing the scene, but then they had an excuse. We didn't. Because, ludicrous as our eastern friends may have looked, what impression did we give? Our three ladies – Pat, Iris and Maggie – were sitting discussing the merits of the dress worn by a lady at a neighbouring table. Bert was studying the fingerwork of the guitar player. Clive was trying to attract the attention of the wine waiter, and I was making mental notes about the tourists! My God, 16 naked women and not a witness to the event.

Such are the ways of human nature. As they say in Yorkshire, 'There's nowt so queer as folk.' How true, and how embarrassing when folk are being queer on your TV show when you're least expecting it. For many years, and many hundreds of TV programmes, I had prided myself on the fact that there was never a situation that couldn't in the end have been transmitted live if push came to shove. But such a happy situation couldn't last – Fate is simply waiting to succumb to that sort of temptation. It got its chance on *Cross Wits*.

My normal procedure with any game show is to chat generally to the guests but never, of course, to discuss the topics we will talk about on air. This prevents the people worrying over how best to reply, how much to embroider the tale, or worst of all to say 'As I was telling you earlier'. Rather, I leave the researchers to find me interesting snippets to discuss, and then cross my fingers. It usually works – but it did not on this particular day. My somewhat cryptic brief was that the guest was interested in photographing gravestones and had once been locked in a cemetery. Good stuff, but not the way it was told to the cameras.

'I gather you were once locked in a cemetery,' I prompted.

'Yes. I didn't know they closed at night and I was locked in, and the mist and darkness were coming down. Very scary.'

'So what did you do?'

'What could I do? I knocked up the vicar's wife!' said the contestant in all innocence.

'Oh, really' was all I could think of while my brain shot off in fifty directions at once. Had he really said what I thought he'd said? Was I sure? What should I do now? Try to carry on. Too late! Audience, camera crew, production team – all were in hysterics. Recording had stopped, but not before they'd captured all the chat and the expression on my face in which blind panic competed with hilarity. I was sent a copy of the tape for Christmas. I watch it from time to time, whenever I'm tempted to know it all.

Audiences and game-show guests are the finest reputation-bashers on earth. They care not for fame, fortune, achievements or position in life. They just say and do the first thing that occurs to them. Sometimes it can be highly embarrassing – as in the case of the monkey. You remember the monkey? You *don't*? You should get out more. I thought the world and his wife knew what happened in Blackpool. We were making a comedy series for the BBC and our producer Rick had decided to have folk from all over Britain telling us true stories in their own dialects. Basically a good idea – but then it had to be improved by some twit we were chatting to in a late-night bar. 'Hey! What about the chimpanzee? That'd look good on your show – it blows a raspberry.' It emerged that there was this baby chimp which would blow a razz if you talked to it. 'What better?' thought Rick. 'You throw it a one-line gag and the chimp reacts.' Funny, would you say? No, I didn't think so either, but who argues with the BBC.

What the airhead at the wine bar neglected to mention was that the animal was a mere week or two old and susceptible to cold. It was a winter's day and we couldn't film indoors, so the chimp was brought out into the freezing air, immediately turned blue, and curled up in a ball. End of filming? No. Brilliant idea: why not sit the chimp on Tom's head. It'll look funny. You're right – it didn't. What happened next was that the frightened baby grabbed me by the cheeks with its rather large finger nails. 'Pull it off,' said Camera 1.

'No, wait!' I protested. Too late: the baby was grabbed and dragged away, taking part of my cheek with it. There was I with a largish chunk of skin adrift. Now the panic started.

'How long since your last anti-tetanus?' someone asked.

'I've no idea.'

'Hospital then – straight away.'

'Phone them up front and warn them to keep it quiet. We'll leave by the back door.' The mumbling went on.

Off I was whisked to the local hospital and quickly and quietly ushered into a back room, where I was greeted by a charming lady about 60 years old.

'You know where you have the jab don't you?' she asked.

'Yes, indeed,' I said, knowing it had to be in the buttocks, because when your luck's out your luck's out.

'OK. Get ready. I won't be a moment.'

Off she went, while I dropped my pants and underpants and prepared to bend over a table. At that precise second, the door opened and my nurse returned, accompanied by four others.

'See, I told you it was him,' she said. 'Oh, by the way, please roll up your sleeve.'

I've never gone so red in my life. I mean red all over!

I wouldn't say I've been plagued by medical problems, but they occasionally follow me about, sometimes with strange consequences. Even when things appear to be totally under control I somehow suffer the most peculiar spin offs. Anybody who has suffered a broken rib knows how unfunny, indeed how excruciatingly painful, it is. I broke three after falling off a horse doing a TV stunt and was strapped up like a chicken by a local doctor. My manager at the time, Tony, came with me and was so upset by the whole affair that he had to drink the large brandy that had been brought for me! Still, it stopped him talking about cancelling engagements until I was better. So off to Guernsey we flew – Pat, Tony, the kids and I – to do two shows, Tuesday and Thursday, with a one night stand in Jersey in between. Because of my frail condition a wheelchair was provided at Heathrow and Guernsey and the same was arranged for the Wednesday flight as well.

Tony is the world's worst flier. He gets drunk at airports

even if he's only seeing people off. So imagine his alarm when he spotted the plane taking us to Jersey: a Trislander, aka the flying banana! A bright yellow eighteen-seater, it was so narrow that passengers sat in twos with no aisle – and therefore no steward service.

'Shove in, Tony,' I said.

'I'm already there,' he replied. And then, turning paler by the second, he cried out: 'My God, the pilot's wearing an overcoat and gloves!'

'So what?'

'So get me a large drink right away. Get the steward!'

'No steward, Tony.'

'I'll drink my own.'

And he did: fourteen miniatures which he had in his bag; whisky, vodka, brandy – anything that might, however briefly, engender a feeling of equanimity – or at least fatalism. Twenty minutes, fourteen miniatures – not bad going. The only trouble was, when we disembarked Tony found he couldn't stand up. We prised him out of the plane, and he was conveyed to a taxi in the wheelchair intended for me. Dear God, how we artistes suffer for our managers! Still, he did save us a few bob on that trip by demanding special attention at the hotel.

'The man is extremely ill and must have a good night's sleep. Please find him a quiet room,' Tony told the manager.

'Understood, sir.'

'I know there's refurbishment going on, and I don't mind a noisy room, but Mr O'Connor *must* have peace and quiet.'

'Of course, Sir. I understand.'

Maybe he did understand, maybe he didn't. But he didn't give me a quiet room – in fact, it turned out to be noisier than Tony's! Drills, saws, hammers, whistling, singing – I had all that at 7.30 am, and there I lay unable to sit up without assistance. Tony came in about 9.00 am and when he heard the racket he went ape.

'Is that Reception? Listen to this noise,' he shouted, and

held out the phone to pick up the sounds of the workmen.
He even called in a chambermaid to hear for herself. It
worked, the receptionist was so apologetic she insisted we
take a 25 per cent cut in our bill. As we left the desk, the
assistant manager approached us and wouldn't hear of our
leaving until we took a further 25 per cent cut in our bill.
He was followed by the actual manager who again gave us
a 25 per cent deduction.

'My God,' said Tony. 'If we stay here any longer we'll
be making a profit.'

In showbusiness, one thing I've learnt is that nobody is
ever bigger than the job he's doing – especially if that job
is at Carnegie Hall, New York! It was St Patrick's Week
and I was appearing with the Fureys and, amazingly, doing
a storm before a full house of Irish and Americans. What a
show! The Fureys stood them up, sat them down and stood
them up again. It was all a great introduction to America
for me and I'm forever grateful to Maggie Cadden, Finbar
and the boys for all their kindness. I tried to express this to
them personally at the party afterwards. This was held at
Kennedy's bar – a terrific restaurant–bar complex where we
adjourned at 6.00 pm for a meal and a gentle wind down
amongst family, friends, and members of our audience.

Charlie Comer, the greatest publicist in the world (and
an exiled Scouser) made a pact with me: if I sang 'When
your old wedding ring was new', then he'd sing a song too.
I enlisted the help of the house pianist and we made a fairly
good fist of the number. So much so that a diner asked if I
would sing a request song: 'Danny Boy'.

'Delighted,' I smiled. We belted it out at mega-decibels,
and followed it with 'Delilah', 'My mother's eyes' and a
few more. When eventually I yielded to pressure from
Charlie to let him have the mike, I was approached by the
'Danny Boy' diner:

'Many thanks,' he said – and slipped ten dollars into my
palm. He didn't know who I was, he hadn't been to the

show, he thought I was the house singer! Strangely enough, he made my day. He didn't look drunk, so there was no excuse! I genuinely must have sounded OK – and boy, you can't imagine how good that made me feel. All in all, a one-off occasion. But they're the best, aren't they? Ask Lennie Bennett.

As a bit of an expert on ad libs, I reckon Lennie must rate in the top three I've ever heard. To start with, you've got to give him bonus points for choosing the venue, the London Palladium, which was the top venue of a tour starring the singer Jack Jones and featuring Lennie as the warm-up act. I should explain at the outset that Jack Jones audiences have a tendency not to be interested in any other act but him. So it is not unusual for the bulk of them to stay out of the auditorium during the first half, only taking their seats at the interval, ready for Jack in the second half.

On this particular night all was as normal, Lennie working to a house barely half full, with the rest of the punters outside in the foyer bar. Ten minutes into his patter, Lennie spotted a man moving towards the stage. The punter had realised there were seats nearer the front and he was making his way towards them, clambering over the rows in between.

'What are you doing?' enquired a bemused Bennett.

'I am coming to the front,' replied the man in a very guttural accent.

'Where are you from?' asked Lennie.

'Hamburg,' came the reply.

'That's all I bloody need,' sighed Bennett, 'a German hurdler.' I know Len, I understand, I sympathise – but I wish I'd thought of the line. Many's a night I've been in need of a line like that and it's not been forthcoming, many's the time I've stood stunned, mouth agape and prayed for just one good line.

Only recently at the Albert Hall I could have used a quick quip, although even that might not have saved the day. I was compèring a musical concert and had to announce a very brilliant composer/conductor. To make his entrance the easier, I decided to brief him on matters logistical.

'On your way to the rostrum, sir, there is a six inch step down. I've marked it in white gaffer tape so that you can't miss it. But do be aware after the piece you're conducting you'll have to step up six inches to get off.'

'Thank you, my good man, leave it to me.'

I left it to him – guess what happened. Going on he stepped down beautifully. Fourteen minutes later, he took his bows and strode off, stepping up six inches beautifully. And then, would you believe it, he walked straight through the drum kit. Cymbals, bells, side drums, bass drum, sticks, drummer – the whole works were scattered to all parts. The crowd stared, aghast. I scrambled for a good one liner, missed it by miles, shrugged my shoulders, and announced the interval!

Having mentioned enough of my own disasters, let me close the chapter on a happier note: a disaster that happened to someone else! Who was it who said: 'To succeed is not enough: others must appear to have failed.'

The hero, or fall guy, of this cautionary tale is still alive and working well and very often, so he shall remain nameless. His story is one which could have happened to anyone, anytime and they might have escaped with nothing but credit. In the case of our man, he started badly and just faded away. It's no fun to be brought in as a replacement for an artiste whose show is so distinctively successful that it would be almost unthinkable without him. Bob Monkhouse and *Celebrity Squares* or Jim Bowen and *Bullseye* go together like salt and pepper, peaches and cream. So it was with Bruce Forsyth and *Sunday Night at the London Palladium*, that massive, long-running hit show of a few years ago. Imagine being brought in to host one edition of the show that Bruce couldn't do. Worse still is the fact that you're not a stand-up comic, used to living on his wits, but a fine comedy actor who relies on others' words for his ammunition. Nervous was not the word for our debutante, and the producer decided to boost everybody's confidence by slipping the actor a couple of stiff Scotches. The procedure for the stand-in was simple: opening a couple of minutes' patter (all read from cue cards), announce girl singer, take her off, and announce juggler. Then straight into end of part one. Game show in Part Two: 'Beat the Clock'. Part Three, announce the top of the bill, Rosemary Clooney – a giant star at the time.

So, armed with several Scotches, our man went live on TV, read the gags and received roars of laughter. Confidently he announced the girl, followed that with the juggler and coasted neatly on to the break – and a couple more large ones.

'The phones haven't stopped,' screamed the exultant producer. 'You're an instant hit – you're another Bruce Forsyth. Have another jar.'

'I'll have a double if you don't mind,' smiled our man.

On to Part Two and the guest couple went into a storming edition of the quiz game and won the star prize. Huge applause. More fun and 'falling-down liquid' in the second commercial break, and our man was feeling no pain. Now it was all down to auto pilot, then goodnight and goodbye. Well, not quite. The game show had finished earlier than scheduled, and the producer said to our hero:

'We need to fill in two minutes before you announce Rosemary. There's no time to write out any gags, so just jolly them along with a few jokes of your own. OK?'

'OK,' mumbled a bemused actor, who began desperately dredging his brain for a couple of gags suitable for a family audience.

Out on TV, live to the masses, staggered a terrified compère. What he'd forgotten was that he'd been entertaining the audience for 40 minutes and they loved him. Anything he said they'd laugh at. So he hit them with all the old gags – old but gold – and did a storm. Now all he had to do was to announce ... announce ... Jesus Christ, what's the woman's name? Gamely he pressed on with his introductory patter:

'Ladies and gentlemen, it's star time at the London Palladium and here is a lady who is a star not only in England, not only in America, but all over the world ... In Egypt, Singapore, Hong Kong ...' and still his brain refused to come up with the name. 'You want to see her, the folks at home want to see her, the world wants to see her,' he waffled. By this time Miss Clooney's piano player perceived that something hideous was impending, and he began playing 'This old house', Rosemary's mega-hit. Still no spark from the compère. And after three long, long minutes live on TV, he actually said:

'You know her, and I know her' and, turning to the pianist, he said 'Who is she?'

'Rosemary Clooney,' said the accompanist in a strangled voice.

'See, even *he* knows her,' said our man as the shebang slithered into farce. He was never seen on TV again, but his one night of glory still shines out as a warning light to all would-be overnight successes. When watching experts like Forsyth and Monkhouse, always remember that just 'cos it looks easy, doesn't mean it is easy. Otherwise everybody would be doing it!

17

By jove, is it as late as that?

Have we finally reached the end of this particular road? It hardly seems two ticks since I was casting my mind back to childhood days and 'the way we were', and here we are fifty years later looking back at all the fun I've seen and the places I've been. Hard to believe that my modest beginnings would lead me to some of the most exciting places on earth, rubbing shoulders with some of the greatest stars. Many a time I stare down a golf fairway and picture the little dark-haired nipper with the scruffy shoes and a hole in the seat of his trousers and wonder how it all went right. No doubt about it, luck is the major element in the transformation. Luck, the hand of God, good friends and the most important factor of all – a loyal and loving family.

Without my lovely Pat I would be nowhere in sight. Her encouragement, love and dedication are worth more than all the standing ovations and momentous nights I've had. Money, fame, experience, reputation – all are nothing compared to the love of my life and her happiness. Without our children, and the need to feed them, I wouldn't even be a singer in a pub – I'd probably be a bored and boring deputy headmaster whose clothes and brain were both clogged with chalk dust. Without the audiences, agents and promoters who for some reason liked my act, where would I be?

Likewise my career resulted from the faith of TV and radio producers – sometimes committing themselves to me against all the odds. To all, and to every person who has been involved in my career, both actively and passively, I give thanks. Because of them we go on, year after year, with no thought of retirement or even easing back on the work.

A family of children has grown up and been succeeded by a family of grandchildren, who come everywhere with Pat and me when they can. Butlins, Haven, Warner, cruises – all heaven-sent venues for eager-eyed youngsters. Pantomimes are even more exciting – even on a noisy day I can detect my own family out in the audience – booing, cheering, clapping, shouting on cue.

Along with the obvious satisfaction of having a happy family around me, I've an awful lot to be thankful for. Once, when I was being interviewed on radio, I was asked what age of all that I'd experienced would I like to be now. To tell you the truth my answer surprised even me, but it still holds good. I honestly wouldn't swap any age for what I am now. Never in my life have I been so happy. Look at it from my position. I love entertaining people and I love playing golf. I now get paid to do both – guest speaker at golf dinners, family entertainer, quiz host – you name it and I get the chance to do it (or not, if I so choose). So shake hands with a happy man, a man who, given the chance, wouldn't change any part of his life – but also a man who is aware that, without change, nothing can prosper for long.

So what next? Which new avenue is to be explored? Which new test of the grey matter and the nerves will the management dream up? Well, let's look at the options and maybe you can help me decide.

A wise man once rashly stated that every comedian wants to play Hamlet. Not true, I'm sure – certainly not true for this comic. Quite apart from anything else, there are very few pattermen who would want to be restrained by words and timing to the same performance every night. Even pantomime gives the talker the chance to ad lib or at least to change the script to suit that night's audience or take advantage of that day's headlines. No, the funny man does not necessarily want to switch to tragedy, although that isn't to say that the opposite applies to the straight actor. Remember the story of the hard-up thespian who was tramping the boards with a very poor touring company. The rumour went round the theatre that Bernard Delfont was in the audience looking for actors for an extraordinarily long run of pantomime. On went the hungry ham, and delivered those unforgettable words:

'To be or not to be, that is the question. Oh no it isn't!'

On the other hand, I do like to combine a little acting with my normal chat. A year or so ago I had the pleasure of playing a straight-ish role in *Perils of the Pond*, a super play written for and acted by children, in which I had the role of Pike, the villain of the piece. How difficult I found it! Not so much getting into the character, but witnessing the shock and fear on the young faces in the audience as I suddenly appeared in a cloud of dark smoke from the trap door – green face, green hair, horrible features. The reaction was the opposite of what I had experienced all my professional life, and to tell you the truth I didn't enjoy it. I'd be happier playing a comedy part, of course. At least I'd be expecting laughter and the only constraint would be having to keep to the exact words of the script. So maybe a TV sitcom would be an idea to consider.

Believe it or not, singing may even come into the frame for consideration. As if the whole world had gone full circle, the tours of Ireland I've been on have become so regular that it has been necessary to vary the content of the act. Always the most difficult part is the ending – getting off is an art. So more and more I've been introducing music to ease my way through an hour's cabaret. Of course the Irish love songs and singing – even mine. So perhaps something musical – a record, or even an album – could be considered.

What about a video featuring my comedy skills, with a little music as well? Good idea and one which we're contemplating doing this year, with one eye on follow-up releases if we get the initial blueprint right. Having video material to play on TV is an ideal way to help break into other countries. America, Australia, South Africa and all the other English-speaking nations are wide open for tours provided the name is broadcast up front, so ready-recorded material is always a useful thing to have in store.

So far all my thoughts for the future have been to do with work. But what about a different future in which I might abandon showbusiness for other pursuits. Well, there's one other vocation that certainly appeals to me. Having missed a huge part of my children's younger days because of work schedules, I find I'm very reluctant to miss the same period of my grandchildren's lives. That's the reason why this tired old comic makes his way home through the night on Saturday to see the kids, albeit through sleepy eyes, on Sunday. Yes, I'm determined to do certain things from now on. The most important is to be a complete grandparent – and to do that takes a lot of hard work. Ask any child what is required of grandparents and they will give you a clue as to how complex the role is. 'God made grandparents 'cos he can't be everywhere at once,' was one child's explanation. Another complained, 'Grandfathers insist on showing you how to play football – even when you're a girl!'

So part one of the future is learning to be a good grandad and enjoying the company of young minds, and I suppose part two will have to be a mental challenge just to keep the old head from falling off. I've decided to look for the world's best joke. Strange idea I know, but it would balance out my first ever book, which was called *The World's Worst Jokes* and featured some stupefyingly dire stuff – too bad even for my act. So the best joke has more appeal. But is there such a thing? Is there one, and only one, anecdote which can reduce every audience to quivering wrecks? I've never found one, although on some nights I've been near, but then that could have been the drink. When would I deliver it? At the start of the act? After two or three minutes? At the end? You see, timing is all important.

Would it be a family gag like:

Husband, sitting next to wife who is driving very erratically, 'What are you doing?'

'I've lost control, I can't stop it, what'll I do?'

'Brace yourself and hit something cheap!'

Would it be an Irish Joke like:

Two Irish fellas found a dead animal and began to argue.

'It's a donkey.'

'No, no it's a mule.'

The parish priest came past and they asked:

'Father, is this a donkey or a mule?'

'Neither,' said he. 'It's an ass, and don't leave it here — bury it.'

As they dug away with shovels, a pal arrived saying:

'What are you digging, lads — a fox hole?'

'Not according to the parish priest,' they replied.

You see, I'm not sure any of these gags or any gag I've ever heard would stand up entirely on its own. I mean, it would need an unusual opening, an interesting middle and a blinding finish that wasn't expected, and I can't think of a solitary joke that has that. Except, maybe, the one about the bloke who goes into the pet shop and.... Here, wait a minute — you've heard that one before, haven't you?

☐	From the Wood to the Tees	Tom O'Connor	£4.99
☐	One Flew Over the Clubhouse	Tom O'Connor	£4.99
☐	How Was It For You	Maureen Lipman	£4.50
☐	Something to Fall Back On	Maureen Lipman	£4.50
☐	Thank You for Having Me	Maureen Lipman	£4.50
☐	When's It Coming Out?	Maureen Lipman	£4.99
☐	George – Don't Do That	Joyce Grenfell	£4.50
☐	Stately as a Galleon	Joyce Grenfell	£3.99
☐	Turn Back the Clock	Joyce Grenfell	£5.99

Warner Books now offers an exciting range of quality titles by both established and new authors. All of the books in this series are available from:

Little, Brown and Company (UK),
P.O. Box 11,
Falmouth,
Cornwall TR10 9EN.

Alternatively you may fax your order to the above address. Fax No. 01326 317444.

Payments can be made as follows: cheque, postal order (payable to Little, Brown and Company) or by credit cards, Visa/Access. Do not send cash or currency. UK customers and B.F.P.O. please allow £1.00 for postage and packing for the first book, plus 50p for the second book, plus 30p for each additional book up to a maximum charge of £3.00 (7 books plus).

Overseas customers including Ireland please allow £2.00 for the first book plus £1.00 for the second book, plus 50p for each additional book.

NAME (Block Letters) ....

....

ADDRESS ....

....

....

☐ I enclose my remittance for ....

☐ I wish to pay by Access/Visa Card

Number ⬚⬚⬚⬚⬚⬚⬚⬚⬚⬚⬚⬚⬚⬚⬚⬚

Card Expiry Date ⬚⬚⬚⬚